DR. JAMES CURTIS HEPBURN
At 95 years

Hepburn of Japan

and His Wife and Helpmates

A Life Story of Toil for Christ

By

William Elliot Griffis, D.D., L.H.D.

Author of "The Mikado's Empire," "Brave Little
Holland," "Verbeck of Japan," and
"A Modern Pioneer in Korea"

The Westminster Press
Philadelphia
1913

THE·PLIMPTON·PRESS
NORWOOD·MASS·U·S·A

DEDICATED
IN SINCERE APPRECIATION OF THE
SECOND GENERATION OF CHRISTIAN MISSIONARIES
IN JAPAN
ESPECIALLY TO THE SONS AND DAUGHTERS
WHO THRUST IN THE SICKLE
WHERE THEIR PARENTS CAST IN THE SEED

NISI DOMINUS FRUSTRA

PREFACE

OF the four great pioneers of the gospel and Christian civilization in Japan, Verbeck, Brown, Hepburn and Williams, this volume completes the biography of that one who was second on the ground and possibly the first in general usefulness. America's greatest gift to Japan was in these men. I knew them all, during four years in the Mikado's empire, as neighbors, friends and fellow workers, in perils and in joys. Though not technically a missionary — my calling being that of an educational pioneer — I loved and rejoiced in their work, as if one of them. From 1870 until Dr. Hepburn's decease in 1911, we were always friends, and also occasional correspondents.

But without that noble work of God, the "help meet for him," there would have been no such Dr. Hepburn, as all Japan and we his friends knew, and so I have in this volume much to say about Mrs. Hepburn.

She wrote me, on March 21, 1895, concerning her husband, as follows:

"I think you have understood him. His modest, unselfish life leads him more and more to keep in the

PREFACE

background. The work he has been permitted to do for his dear Master has brought its own reward. I think he might adopt the words of Bonar, 'The things we have lived for, let them be our story, and we be best remembered by what we have done.' . . . If anyone is to write of Dr. Hepburn, when his work is done, I know of no one I would rather should do it than yourself."

So, after the Doctor's decease, at the invitation and request of his only son, Mr. Samuel Hepburn, who, in his father's home, showed me, and afterwards sent, all the available diaries and documents left by his father, I took up the congenial task of sketching the life of my friend — a true American to the backbone, a loyal samurai of Jesus, a lover of all mankind. Amid many labors pressing upon me, this particular one has afforded indescribable pleasure, in living over old days in the Princess country. I have enjoyed telling also about some of the Doctor's fellow Christian samurai, as loyal to their divine Master as he was. Dai Nippon's shining record of noble characters is rich, but none have exceeded in the graces of true chivalry, in real courage, and in the loftiest phases of Bushido, the Christian leaders of the New Japan. Laus Deo!

My Japanese friends must excuse me for clinging to the ancient and honorable term Mikado — symbol of all things great in Japanese history and radiant with the undimmed luster of ages. I have never quite forgiven them for dropping this august native

PREFACE

term, and adopting in its place the Latin expression, "Emperor," which, to a true American, savors of despotism and even cruelty, which has been linked with many unsavory historical associations and upon which no genuine American can lavish respect. If, also, I say "native" when I mean Japanese, it is because in our land we are not ashamed of the word, and also because the English language has its rights.

From Hepburn may there ever be in Japan a true apostolical succession of zealous, loyal, diligent and self-effacing servants of Jesus.

W. E. G.

ITHACA, N. Y.
  Era of Taisei, first year, sixth month, thirty-first day.
            A.D. 1913, March 31.

CONTENTS

LIST OF ILLUSTRATIONS

Hepburn of Japan
and His Wife and Helpmates

Hepburn of Japan
and His Wife and Helpmates

INTRODUCTION

SEEN IN PERSPECTIVE

PERRY won political Japan from a hermit life, but Hepburn opened the Japanese heart. Townsend Harris began the commercial, and American missionaries the educational, invasion of the Mikado's empire.

When on September 22, 1911, the newspapers of Japan printed with headlines this official telegram sent by Baron Uchida, the Mikado's ambassador at Washington:

Dr. James Curtis Hepburn died Thursday morning, December 21, 1911,

there were some who wondered why this message was sent. How was it, that while great and notable men in America might pass away without official notice, a private citizen in New Jersey should be thus honored?

In Japan, a sense of grief, with sincere mourning, as of the loss of the nation's best foreign friend, pervaded the court and nation. All over the empire

[3]

the press, taking up the refrain, printed the news, and made extended explanation and commentary.

Old residents of Nippon, from many countries of Europe or America, or those returned home from former labors, had no need of any explanation; while among the natives at large, but more especially in eastern Japan, myriads of people would have felt insulted if asked whether they could tell who their dear Dr. Hepburn was. "Kun-shi" — the superior man, the gentleman, was the word of affectionate admiration which came at once to their lips. Thousands, living, gratefully remembered him as the kind physician who had healed their diseases, and perhaps restored their eyesight. Others, of the newer generation, recalled the beaming countenances and tones of reverent gratitude, in parents or grandparents, who had been healed or helped by the American, whose name was to them as a household word. Added to these were Japanese ambassadors, statesmen and leading men in the social and commercial world, who had known the Doctor as their friend, neighbor, or teacher. Throughout the membership of the medical and scientific bodies of educated men, in Tokyo and elsewhere, there was a keen sense of personal loss, even while they paid tribute to this pioneer of science in the Land of Peaceful Shores.

Especially in the Christian churches was memory active. Many were the joyous reminiscences, public memorial meetings, interchanges by word and letter, and tributes in various forms, to one long called in

[4]

popular estimation "The Nation's Friend." In the Sunny Isles the memory of Hepburn is as enduring as are the evergreens on the richly clad mountains.

When the pilgrim had left behind him earthly cares for his long home, he had seen all but three of the years of a century. One may divide his life's record into five parts: (1) the training in youth and early manhood, which fitted him to be a healer of the bodies and souls of men (1815–1840); (2) his career as a missionary physician, in China and the Far East, when the Middle Kingdom was inhospitable and Japan was as yet a sealed book (1840–1846); (3) his work as practicing physician in New York City (1846–1859); (4) his later service of thirty-three years as teacher, healer, lexicographer, translator, saint and father, in the Mikado's empire (1859–1892); and (5) his nineteen years in the sunny afternoon of life, as church officer and philanthropist at East Orange, New Jersey, (1892–1911).

Hepburn was a wonderful man, yet in some respects a unique character. By temperament as timid as a child, he was, in facing difficulties, as bold as a knight in steel. Again and again have I heard him talk, in the face of some great danger or problem, as if under deep forebodings of disaster. One would think, in listening to him talk of himself, that he had hardly the courage of a kitten. Yet he never feared the assassin or his blade, and in real valor outshone the samurai with his brace of swords. Those who knew his clear vision of God, his keen sense of the heavenly

Father's abiding presence and his trust in the literal reality of the divine promises, never expected Hepburn to flinch when any lion of danger stood in the way. Nor were they disappointed. Armed with the strength of God, this man of faith knew no fear. His trust in the eternal Reality increased and his courage grew with years. Long experience taught him that most of life's troubles, when one faces them boldly, are imaginary, and that to the Christian, the powers that fight for the child of God and for righteousness are ever greater than those arrayed against truth and them that believe. The "mountain sides," in Hepburn's landscape of faith, were ever "white with many an angel tent."

So it actually came to pass that this timid, shrinking gentleman, this "little dried-up old man" as some thought of him — and the words are his own — was an absolutely fearless soldier, when the bugles of duty sounded. More than this, he was an inspiration to others, ever effective to "strengthen the wavering line."

Hepburn knew — and I have heard him joke about it — that his physical frame was slight and his health far from robust. In fact, he chuckled at the truth contained in the funny words of Dr. Oliver Wendell Holmes — a "little old gentleman" like himself — as well as in those of Scripture, that in the long run of life, "the race is not to the swift or the battle to the strong." The Yankee healer once wrote out a sure receipt for longevity. In effect, it prescribed that a man should have some incurable disease; so that, while the physicians were chronically at work, feeling his pulse and pounding his lungs to sound them, the patient would take care of himself and live to a good old age. Meanwhile, the undertakers might grow prosperous because men who boasted of their "iron constitution" were called away often and early. It was once said of a Schenectady clergyman, by a learned professor in Union College, that he "would always have something the matter with him, and yet outlive us all." So Dr. Hepburn, starting in life without robustness and apparently always afflicted more or less with physical troubles of some kind, died at the age of ninety-seven. I remember that he complained of his ills only when we could direct the conversation upon himself — never otherwise. Not a few of his letters tell the tale of a variety of physical discomforts borne patiently.

Nineteen years before he passed away, he wrote in one of his many letters to me: "I am just about to make a journey to Germany with my wife, seeking for health. I have been suffering for the last three years with neuralgia and rheumatism in my back and legs, so as to be quite disabled from walking more than a short distance. Every spring, for three years past, it seems to have attacked my feet, this spring with increased severity, so that I have been laid up now in the house and not able to put on anything but the loosest slipper for nearly five weeks."

At another time, when about ninety years of age, he wrote, telling me of the woes that had come to him from the grippe. All his previous pains seemed to have concentrated in his head, while suffering from "a misfit skull." Yet seven years more of life were borne with a merry twinkle in his eye.

All this reveals the fact that this superb knight of God, this samurai of Jesus, obtained his greatest triumphs over himself. Gigantic as might have seemed the difficulties from without, he was a victor over the infirmities within. His mastery of Malay and Chinese, his wrestling with an insular language, when no grammar nor dictionary existed, the compiling of a colossal dictionary, the translation of the divine Word into a tongue but ill fitted for spiritual treasures, his work as oculist, surgeon and medical factotum, the daily drudgery of the dispensary, and the bearing of the burdens of a pastor — in fact, though not in name — all these were victories won outside of himself, while all the time his chief triumph was over himself.

There was little in Hepburn's temperament, for example, like that of Appenzeller of Korea, Verbeck of Japan, or S. R. Brown, "a maker of the New Orient." In fascinating variety and strong contrast were the personalities of such giants in the missionary pioneer work, as Legge, Williamson, McCartee, Nathan Brown, Williams, Greene, and others, whom the writer knew intimately, and with a familiarity that bred no contempt. Most superbly does Providence fit men for their work and put each into his niche.

In his cast of mind, Hepburn was severely conservative. Despite his amazing industry and constant discipline of service, he never entered into the world of modern criticism. His erudition and scholarship, wonderful as they were, can hardly be said to have passed into the promised land of the most modern science, or of critical history, or of that theology, which, based on the direct teaching of Jesus, is rapidly freeing itself from merely scholastic and medieval trammels. Yet Hepburn's insight into the eternal truths was something quite independent both of any opinions in any particular era in the world's history, or of a temperament based on physical accidents of heredity or environment. Ever seeking his life out of himself in God, he was apparently indifferent to changing views and opinions, even while kindly tolerant to those who differed from him. With the ignorant, conceited, or impetuous, instead of magisterial haughtiness, he held rather the attitude of a discerning physician of souls.

In 1881, as he wrote me: "The Christian work (in Japan) moves on under many difficulties. Some of our native pastors give us much trouble and anxiety. There is still the old dislike for foreigners and a desire to manage things themselves, not knowing that they are ignorant, narrow-minded, and that self reigns within them. Christianity will have to fight a battle here of peculiar character."

[9]

Verily Hepburn was a seer and a prophet!

Ever full of cheer and encouragement, he was far from being a flatterer, and the best natives appreciated this. One of the best traits of the Japanese is that, when honest men, who detest flattery and cajolery — men in whom they trust — show them their faults, they in the long run learn to set high value upon the judgment of their critical friends. "Not joyous but grievous," such wholesome truth-telling in the end, "yieldeth peaceable fruit unto them that have been exercised thereby, even the fruit of righteousness."

Clad in a mantle of intense moral courage, wrought of the finest fiber, in the looms of a profound spirituality, Hepburn illustrated what a famous Puritan woman said of her husband, Col. Hutchinson:

"It was indeed a great instruction that the best and highest courages are but the beams of the Almighty; and when he withholds his influence the brave turn cowards, fear unnerves the most mighty, makes the most generous base, and great men to do those things they blush to think on when God again inspires; the fearful and the feeble see no dangers, believe no difficulties, and carry on the attempt, whose very thought would at another time shiver their joints like ague."

With Hepburn, life was "the energy of Love."

I

A HAPPY BOYHOOD

JAMES CURTIS HEPBURN came of Scotch-Irish stock on his father's side and of English stock on his mother's side. Samuel Hepburn, his great-grandfather, left Belfast, Ireland, in May, 1773. Having emigrated with his family to America, he settled in 1784 at Northumberland, Pennsylvania, where he died in 1795, at the age of 97.

His son, James Hepburn, born in Belfast, March 28, 1747, married Mary Hopewell of Mount Holly, New Jersey, in 1781, and died in Northumberland, Pennsylvania, in 1817, leaving three daughters and seven sons; of whom Samuel, the father of the missionary physician, was the eldest. Samuel was born in Philadelphia in 1782, and died at Lock Haven, Pennsylvania, in 1865.

He was graduated at Princeton College in 1803 and made his home in Milton, Pennsylvania, until a few years before his death, when he removed to Lock Haven. As a citizen and lawyer, he was well known and highly respected. He married Ann Clay, daughter of Rev. Slaytor Clay, of whom one may read a brief notice in Sprague's Annals of the American

Pulpit, Vol. V, p. 355. Of this union were born five daughters and two sons, the oldest son and next oldest of the children being the future benefactor of Japan. Another son, the Rev. Slaytor Clay Hepburn, was long pastor of a Presbyterian church, at Hamptonburgh, Orange County, New York.

The future missionary, born at Milton, Pennsylvania, on March 13, 1815, was brought up in his birthplace. His home was his first and best school and his mother the teacher of teachers to him.

How he was trained in the home the Doctor told himself, in a letter to the biographer, in 1881.

"My father and mother were both humble Christians, bringing up their children (five daughters and two sons) to fear God, to respect and love the Sabbath day, to go to church, to read the Bible and commit to memory the Shorter Catechism. My mother was especially interested in foreign missions. She took the 'Missionary Herald' and the 'New York Observer,' as far back as I can remember. I always read these papers with interest. In these early days, while a boy, I sat under the ministry of Rev. George Junkin, a most earnest, godly man and zealous in every good work."

"Curtis," as his wife always, in later years at least, called him, was fortunate in his teachers. This was the day of the American academies, which trained so many men for public and professional life. The Milton Academy was then under the care of the Rev. David Kirkpatrick, an Irishman, and a graduate of the University of Edinburgh. While under his care, the Milton Academy, a celebrated institution, sent forth many of those who became some of the most distinguished men of the Keystone State.

Men went to college early in those days, and at fourteen James Curtis was ready for Princeton. In the spring of 1831, he made his journey to the college of New Jersey by stage—there being no railways. He was graduated in the autumn of 1832 when "so young as to lose most of the advantages of a college education," as the doctor wrote me in 1881.

It took seventy-two hours to travel from Milton to Princeton, which then had five or six college buildings, the main building, Nassau Hall, being a dormitory. "There was a dining hall in another building, where all the students had their meals. There were two tables, a different price of board being charged at each. There were no eating clubs and none of the students lived in the village, unless his home was there. Young men who could go to college in those days considered themselves fortunate and few wasted their time."

The idea of young Hepburn's parents in sending him to college was, almost as a matter of course, to fit their son to be a Presbyterian minister, as their other son, Slaytor, became. We shall see what became of this plan. Let the Doctor now tell of his experiences while in Princeton College, of which in later life he was for many years "the oldest living graduate."

II

LIFE AT PRINCETON COLLEGE

YOUNG HEPBURN entered when the junior class was half advanced, "was without much ambition and was overshadowed by much older and maturer men." The last term of the senior year was lost by the breaking out of Asiatic cholera in New York and at Princeton, causing a suspension of studies and the closing of the college.

"Yet this short period of college life," said Dr. Hepburn, "was useful in many other ways, especially in bringing me into contact with young men of various types and degrees of culture from all parts of our country, with some of whom I contracted warm and lifelong friendships. I was under the direct personal influence of such men as Professor Albert B. Dod and J. Addison Alexander." All his life, he kept up his knowledge of Greek and Latin and added to this a knowledge of Hebrew sufficient to help him in his work of translating the Old Testament.

His experiences at Princeton marked one of the most eventful periods of his life, for in the spring of 1832, as he said, "I awoke to a new life and was born again of the Spirit." Here, also, through acquaintance with Messrs. Hope and Laird, his mind was turned to the foreign missionary field.

In another interview the nonagenarian said:

"There was no hazing of under-classmen, though some of the secret societies may have followed the custom to a limited degree. One of the most exciting pranks of the time was when a student dropped a torpedo in a stove, in the recitation room of the junior class. The stove was blown to pieces, all the windows were smashed, and some of the benches damaged, but the students were not seriously hurt. The faculty were unable to discover the culprit; but many years afterwards, when Princeton alumni met in New York City, I heard one member of the class — who was at one time a judge of the Supreme Court of New Jersey — admit that he had done it, expecting to hear only a loud report, and not to wreck the room."

During the interview the Doctor referred to the trouble of 1874 between the students of Rutgers College and those of Princeton, when the Rutgers graduates marched from New Brunswick to Princeton, and captured the cannon and carried it away. Something like this had occurred also during the Doctor's college days.

"Most of the students' exercise was taken in walking," the Doctor continued. "Baseball as played to-day was then unknown, but cricket was very common. There were no intercollegiate sports. We got plenty of exercise by walking. A favorite walk, with many of the students, was to a female seminary, about half a mile from the college. If we were fortunate, we got a chance to look at the girls, but seldom had an opportunity to talk to them, as a much stricter watch was kept over young women at that time, especially at boarding schools."

The student's fondness for walking continued throughout his life. At ninety-three years of age the Doctor, after a mile walk, showed little indication of fatigue. He stated his belief that students of the present day sacrifice study for athletics. Possibly his word may help to a saner and healthier life some of those who labor under delusion as to the value of violent exercise. Long observation had shown the physician that the surest way to shorten life is to take a course of overtraining in college athletics, and then stop, when in active business life; while light exercise, kept up as a daily habit, tends to longevity.

"Dr. Ashbel Green had just succeeded President Stanhope Smith, who had done great things for the college in the way of broadening its curriculum — among other things, making provision for regular instruction in chemistry, the first action of the kind ever taken by an American college. From the first, I was deeply interested in this new and comparatively unknown study, and I went into it with all the enthusiasm of a youngster of fourteen.

"In those days, there was in the college requirements a pretty stiff proportion of the classics. I made up my mind that it would be more agreeable to devote some of the time spent on Latin and Greek to chemical experimentation. I agitated the matter a good deal publicly and gained quite a reputation as a kicker. For aught I know, I may have been the original advocate of the elective system.

"In the course of time my critical attitude was brought to the attention of President Green, and he invited me to visit him in his study. 'I hear you have a poor opinion of the Latin and Greek authors,' he said, with a humorous gleam in his eyes. 'What have you discovered that is so out of the way with them?'

"I replied that the only quarrel I had with them was the amount of time they demanded. 'It seems to me that you have an abundance of time,' he replied with a smile. 'You are not yet fifteen, and you have plenty of time to make the acquaintance of these interesting gentlemen.' I replied promptly that I preferred to cultivate the society of the natural scientists.

"Then it was that the president floored me by an argument which convinced me that I had something still to learn. 'How are you going to get to the very bottom of any study, without a knowledge of the classics?' he asked. 'Don't you know that the entire nomenclature of chemistry and much of the literature of the subject are in Latin? How are you going to become eminent in any direction, without a good working knowledge of the classics?'

"President Green's kindness and logic were too

strong a combination to resist, and I went back to my Homer and Livy, determined to give them a chance to do everything they could for me. As it has turned out, I have never made a stir in the world of pure science, but I have found time to produce a Japanese dictionary, which is, I believe, still to be regarded as a standard. I have never regretted that I took President Green's advice."

It would be difficult to see how the great lexicographer's Japanese-English dictionary, on which all others are based, could have been made so excellent without thorough previous linguistic exercise. Hepburn after eight years' labor produced the "golden key between the East and the West." How could he ever have forged, wrought and finished so noble an instrument, at once massive and delicate, without this drill in the classics at Princeton? Great as was Dr. Hepburn's work in the dispensary and at his clinics, and mighty as were the streams of healing which flowed from his hands, his success as Bible translator and dictionary-maker was even more signal. As an oculist, he unsealed many blind eyes, and the lancet in his skillful fingers was mighty in opening the hearts of a once suspicious and inhospitable people. Yet the "Open Sesame," which, in 1867, he spoke, as he alone was able to utter the magic formula, before the hidden cave of the language, opened as nothing else could, or did, the jewel chamber. Over those treasures, the world now rejoices. At his word, the two-leaved gates of the Japanese language and literature swung apart, to the delight of mankind.

Like Gamewell, the missionary and master-engineer in the Peking inclosure, during the Boxer riots of 1900, whose fortifications were the means of preserving the lives of the besieged, Hepburn had at first thought his time wasted on a study in college of what he hardly expected to use. Divine Providence used both the Princeton alumnus and the Cornell graduate to do the work to which unexpected opportunity had in each case given a strenuous call. "For my thoughts are not your thoughts, neither are your ways my ways," saith Jehovah, and very often thought his servant, Dr. Hepburn.

In later life James Curtis Hepburn won as titles the degrees of A.M., from Princeton College, in 1835; M.D., from the University of Pennsylvania, in 1836; LL.D., from Lafayette College, in 1872; and LL.D., from his Alma Mater, in 1904, when over ninety years old. He was also chosen to honorary membership in many learned societies, and was given the decoration of the Order of the Rising Sun, Third Class, from the Mikado of Japan, Mitsuhito the Great.

III

THE GREAT DECISION

HOW the boy, — whom his parents had wished to be a minister, — was disposed by the Holy Spirit to be a physician and a missionary, and how he came to "throw his life away" — as some said in 1840 — only to find it in richness a hundredfold, was narrated by the one chiefly concerned.

"My first serious impressions about personal religion were in the winter of 1831–32 while at Princeton College. There was a revival in the college, and I then began first to think seriously of my relations to God. However, I did not obey the call of the Spirit and give myself to Christ until in the winter of 1834, while attending medical lectures in Philadelphia. I joined the Presbyterian church in Milton, Pennsylvania, that same year."

The father of Curtis would gladly have had his son a lawyer, if the ministry was out of the question; but the young student thought the pleading at the bar would require some oratorical ability; and this he never possessed. By taste and natural fitness, he thought he was marked for the profession of medicine.

[20]

Among his fellow students in Princeton was Richard Armstrong (the father of General Sam Armstrong, long the president of the Hampton Institute), an early missionary to Hawaii. Another was Matthew Laird, who went out to Africa. Both at college and at the medical school a companion who influenced him was Matthew B. Hope, who afterwards went to Singapore as a missionary. "All these influences and associations gave my mind a bias to the foreign missionary work," Dr. Hepburn said, many years later.

In his native town of Milton, he began the study of medicine with Dr. Samuel Pollock and also attended three courses of medical lectures in the University of Pennsylvania at Philadelphia. He received his diploma and the degree of M.D. in the spring of 1836.

Of all the professions, it is probable that the ministry is, on the whole, one of the easiest to enter and one of the hardest in which to keep up. In the medical profession, on the contrary, it is difficult at first to obtain recognition and standing, it is comparatively easy to maintain oneself in practice and reputation in later life; or, at least it was so, in the days before medical science was revolutionized by the discovery of bacteria and the germ theory of disease.

The young doctor, armed with a sheepskin, was, during most of four years very much like Noah's dove — he was ever seeking a rest for the sole of his foot. Not till his second flight away from home, did he pluck the olive leaf that gave joy to others and fixed his own life destiny. He spent one year, 1837, in West Philadelphia, then a thinly settled suburb of the great city between the Delaware and the Schuylkill rivers, but now a part of the city which contains hundreds of thousands of people. Here Dr. Hepburn undertook the duties of a medical friend who was absent.

In the autumn of 1838, he opened an office in Norristown, Pennsylvania. It was here that two of the greatest decisions of his life were made: he determined to be a missionary to heal and help the people of Asia, and he formed a partnership for life with Miss Clarissa Leete, whom the Doctor called Clara.

Of this woman, who was almost as wonderful in her personality as the Doctor himself, only pleasant memories are treasured by scores of Japanese wives and mothers, who enjoyed her teaching as the pioneer educator of women in Japan, as well as by hundreds of United States naval officers who found hospitable cheer in the home of the Hepburns, to say nothing of those to whom, as strangers in a strange land, she was guide, philosopher and friend. Her ancestor, Governor Leete, was one of the heroic men in Connecticut. He had given refuge and succor to certain of the men who, after condemning that royal anarchist, Charles Stuart, to lose his head, had fled to America. His descendant, the father of Miss Clara, had emigrated southward with his daughter to Fayetteville,

North Carolina. Dr. Hepburn met her when she was assisting her cousin — the principal of the Norristown Academy — as a teacher in the school. Soon after the young people were engaged, the Doctor made his life decision as laborer abroad in Christ's name. His betrothed proved to be a true helpmeet for him, for she was ready and willing to go with him.

Back of all other influences leading him to make this decision was the influence of his mother. At the head of a band of women who prayed for the coming of the kingdom, she did not fail to let her son know her own heart's desire concerning him. Nevertheless, when the time came for him to choose, she could hardly bear to have him decide to go to the ends of the earth.

Since 1834 he had been considering the choice. "I did not at first entertain it with pleasure, but more as a stern duty," he said in later life. "My family, especially my father, strongly opposed the idea, and made every effort to turn my mind away from it. I myself tried to cast it off, but I found no rest until I had decided to go. Everything seemed to favor my going — especially finding a wife who was of the same mind and ready to go with me. Although in my first engagement in the foreign missionary work, I had many strong cords to sever which made it exceedingly trying, I found the work itself exceedingly pleasant and congenial."

The decision as to his life work, which was made

despite all protests, was the one which gave to Hepburn the man, a constant and unfailing source of joy during his whole career. I never knew a man who more signally illustrated the dictum of Carlyle: "Blessed is the man that hath found his work. Let him ask no other blessedness." During all his unwearied and ceaseless labors, Dr. Hepburn was sustained by the conviction that he had obeyed the will of God. No matter which way his tastes might run, his sympathies were always in the line of his duty; and because work was his greatest pleasure, he seemed to dignify that work.

One who knew him well wrote to me in 1913: "His one object in life was religion — the Christian religion, and everything he did tended to that sole end. He was of a very retiring disposition, did not care for social life, and — as far as I can judge — he cared for nothing but study and religious subjects."

It was because of this unintermittent, unfailing devotion to duty that some thought him cold-blooded, and certainly he did keep himself unremittingly and systematically at consecrated toil. Yet, probably, those who imagined that this steadiness of habit sprang from merely subjective and temperamental reasons, instead of passionate loyalty to his divine Master, were vastly mistaken. Those who judged him most lightly were they whom the world could most easily spare. It is as certain as mathematics, that Japan became gradually better because, daily from five A.M. to ten P.M., through the thirty-

three years spent within her gates, Dr. Hepburn
kept to his tasks with the tenacity of an ivy vine
to a wall.

There are those who, in view of so strenuous and
fruitful a life as that of Dr. Hepburn, might possibly excuse their own failures or shortcomings, or
at least seek to account for such a career by saying,
"It was natural to him," or, "It was his temperament to be so." Nevertheless, it is certain that the
life story of James Curtis Hepburn is best explained
by deep conviction and overmastering faith. His
own confessions show this. "It is no longer I that
live, but Christ liveth in me," was the declaration
of his mind and heart. "I can do all things in
him that strengtheneth me," was the assured
belief of this constitutionally timid man. Temperament had little to do with it. The Spirit of God and
the loyalty of James Hepburn were the efficient
factors in the noble life of an American whom the
Japanese call "Kun-shi," "a superior man."

After making a journey to Fayetteville, North
Carolina, the lovers were married, on October 27,
1840. The bride and groom expected to sail away
at once, making their bridal trip on the sea, hoping
to begin soon their work in response to the call of the
American Board of Foreign Missions, with which the
Presbyterian churches then coöperated. This call
was for a medical missionary to go out to Siam with
the purpose of working among the Chinese, who
were living in numbers in that country, then newly

opened to American enterprise by treaty; China, a hermit empire, was still closed.

They planned to embark on the ship *United States*, and made hurried preparations to reach Boston in time for her sailing. But these were the days of slow coaches, not of telegraphs or swift trains. When they reached Boston, the vessel had sailed. However, the optimistic doctor saw in this a blessing, for he had seen New England. A few months later, as we shall see, he had further occasion for rejoicing.

The missionaries did not get away until the following March. Then they sailed in an old whaling ship, the *Potomac*.

IV

EASTWARD — A VOYAGE OF THE SOUL

THE long journey over oceans from Boston to Singapore was for the young missionary less one of the body than of the spirit. He was making a great venture of faith. He had time for reflection, for the searching of the spirit, and for the strengthening of his determination. His inner religious experience was deepened. The records in the journal of this voyage explain the whole of his later career, for they reveal the secret springs of his life, more than any other writing of his. Understanding him when on board the ship *Potomac*, we know the man for life.

On the day before his embarkation he wrote in his autograph "Record of a Voyage from Boston to Batavia!"

"Boston, March 14, 1839. Sabbath. — Yesterday was the anniversary of my birth. I am now twenty-six years old. The days of the years of my life are 9491. It is now about six years since I made a profession of religion. If God will reckon with me for every moment of my time — and every moment I am required perfectly to obey his holy law — what must my account be! Twenty years I lived wholly regardless of my obligation to God drinking in iniquity like water, practicing sin and going according to my own lusts, and during the six years, in which I have professed to be a disciple of the Lord, how much of my time has been misspent! Abstracting all that has been ineffective through unbelief, through the force of corruption, through the temptations of the world, that I have trifled away in vain conversation, foolish and wicked thoughts and indolence, how much would there be left! The law of God does not allow a single rebellious or unbelieving thought. It requires us to act always from motives of love to him. It requires truth in the inward parts, purity and holiness. One sin brought death upon the whole human family, death spiritual and temporal, it brought darkness over our souls and shut out the light of life, it brought discord, and corruption amongst our affections."

This passage shows that the young physician was thoroughly imbued with the distinctive doctrines of Calvinism and was strictly orthodox in his belief, as held in the Presbyterian Church. Early instructed in the symbols of the faith, the Westminster Larger and Shorter Catechisms, he held all his life to these bedrocks of faith and order, and, out of them, by the wand of a consecrated will, he brought forth oil for light, wine for exhilaration and water for his soul's refreshment. It was impossible for troubles to beat down or drive back such a man with such a vision.

His clear seeing ever enabled him to discern the superiority of the forces in his favor, so long as he strove to do the will of God, as illustrated in the life of Jesus. Hepburn "seized the triumph from afar," by faith he "brought it nigh."

The passage quoted stands in the light of Hepburn's later life as a true reflector of his innermost spirit. Musing upon his past career, every unconsecrated day of which seemed to him to have been wasted, he made a confession of sin that is not to be taken too literally, except by those whose eyes are open both to the awful nature of sin and to the holiness of God. In this confession, we can see one reason for Hepburn's indomitable industry, of which there was hardly a cessation during fifty years. Many in Japan who knew of the great lexicographer's habits of study and of his drudgery in the dispensary and hospital, realized that he had an iron system, by which every minute was appraised at an eternal value; but not all penetrated the secret of his fruitful and happy life. I have heard some persons speak of him as "a cold-blooded missionary, without sentiment."

Yet even in doing this, they unconsciously paid him their tribute of praise; for, in contrast with others, whose energies were apt to pass too often into the vapor of emotion and sentimentalism, Hepburn was superbly cool. He was inhospitable to "ineffectual emotions." His was not the fear that means cowardice, nor yet the refrigerated caution that savors of the merely mathematical doctrine of averages, and is thus wary in risks; rather was it the fear of God that maketh clean — the purifying fear lest he might flinch from duty.

There were others, who, sharing the intimacy of the untiring student and gentle physician, knew the perfect proportion and the exquisite spiritual beauty of that serene life, "without haste and without rest." Such appraisers of Hepburn's daily round were more accustomed to compare it and the man to a finely tempered blade, that might bend but not break, and whose edge was invincible, when wielded by a ruler of his own spirit. The culture that might seem to the world narrow was in reality profoundly deep and superbly high. In fact, to pursue the metaphor further, Hepburn was a true samurai of Jesus, whose sword was of the Spirit, even the Word of God. As in the ideal of Japanese swordsmanship, the mind and the weapon, the soul and the steel become one in mastery and effect. Possessed of the indwelling power of "the Great Guardian Spirit," the soul of this quiet, forceful man seemed one with his word. The two, lips and life, fitted each other as hand and hilt.

It was on Monday, March 15, 1846, that the stanch ship *Potomac* was all ready to begin her voyage to Java. Besides Captain Carter, who showed himself throughout the whole voyage nobly human in his kindness, sympathy and consideration, there were the first mate Hoyt, the second mate Riddle, and the supercargo Davis, besides a steward, a cook and eleven sailors. Mrs. Hepburn's father, Mr. Lowrie and others, eleven in all, were present to see the missionaries off. Anchor was hoisted at ten o'clock.

Then began what was to the young and delicate wife four months of hardship. The apartment allotted to the travelers was a little cabin, far from being a "state" room. The two bunks were each six by two feet. The endless monotony of food and motion and the unchanging scenes of sea and sky were at times depressing. The creaking of the masts, the dashing of the water against the ship's sides, and, in a gale, the whistling of the wind through the rigging made variety, at least to the ears. Yet the sounds were neither soothing nor alluring.

The bill of fare one day for breakfast was: boiled rice, butter, corn bread, molasses, soused pig's feet, hash and coffee; for dinner, chicken pie, tongue, boiled rice, pickles, turnips, bread pudding and "dip"; for supper, molasses, cold chicken pie, cold ham and hot cakes. A pig was killed every Saturday afternoon. On another day, there was for breakfast soused tripe, rice, etc.; for dinner, roast chicken, salt meat, macaroni, potatoes, turnips, pickles, etc.; for supper, cold chicken, cold meat, toast and gingerbread. There was very little variety in this menu during four months at sea.

From the first, the medical passenger showed himself the friend of all. He was not content with distributing Bibles and tracts to the sailors, who seemed to be grateful for the gifts, for only two out of the eleven possessed a copy of the Scriptures. Besides talking with them, as he had opportunity, he ministered to their physical needs, not only in dispensing medicine, binding up wounds, or poulticing finger felons, but, when necessary, he relieved an aching tooth, or ended its career by extraction. At once he began the study of Malay, for on board was a young man named Eaton, who, though he had forgotten much of his native tongue, was of assistance in pronunciation. Besides sermons and solid works on theology, the Doctor read Milner's Church History, in which he was profoundly interested.

Having only headwork to do while on the ship, the world of living creatures offered him much diversion. He found pleasure in studying the flying fish, the porpoises playing at the bow, the great variety of birds, changing with the latitude, an occasional dolphin and the sea gulls that suggested land. Watching the motions of the clouds as they moved along the horizon, the passengers "felt as if there was something besides themselves in the world."

The contemplation of the ocean gave them "some faint idea of the eternity, power, wisdom and goodness of God. We behold," wrote the Doctor, "evidences of them here as well as in all his other works." Byron has expressed the same thoughts in his immortal verse, in his Childe Harold's Pilgrimage:

> Thou glorious mirror, where the Almighty's form
> Glasses itself in tempests: in all time

Calm or convulsed — in breeze, or gale, or storm,
Icing the pole, or in the torrid clime
Dark-heaving; boundless, endless and sublime;
The image of eternity, the throne
Of the invisible.

On April 10, they passed a Dutch frigate. Its
red, white and blue flag could be discerned with the
eye. With the glass, many heads were noticed looking over the bulwarks at the American ship.

The Bible and their hymn book were the chief
sources of mutual enjoyment. "Our little cabin
becomes our Bethel," is the word picture of the joy
of the young people.

There was little of comfort or luxury on board.
After a while, the drinking water became so bad
that, as the Doctor wrote: "I have to drink it down
like a dose of salts, without tasting it, or cover its
taste by mixing molasses with it. How good would
a glass of cold water from that dear old pump at
home taste now." Yet all these daily discomforts,
borne by homesick knights-errant for God, made them
think less of bodily gratifications and look more to
spiritual joys as the springs of happiness. This
sea experience, based on grim reality, furnished the
principle of life. Ever afterwards, they enjoyed
home comforts all the more.

By April 14 the sun was vertical and woolen clothes
were changed for linen. On April 20, the captain
called attention to the yellow color of the main top-
sail, which he said was owing to a deposit of sand
brought over from the coast of Africa, about five

hundred miles distant, by the northeast trade wind.
The captain declared that on the homeward passage
he had seen the sail likewise colored yellow, when
twelve hundred or more miles away from land.

A shark was caught that had "eyes like a cat"
and plenty of recurved teeth. Its skin was saved
for the making of shagreen — the granulated material
which the Japanese use for ornamenting the hilts of
their swords.

They sailed through whole squadrons of the nau-
tilus, or "Portuguese man-of-war." "The waves
seemed to capsize the tiny sail, but it was soon righted
again and went along, dancing over the banks of the
mighty billows. Another specimen and manifesta-
tion of the works of God, which are all made in
wisdom both in their construction and the end."

On April 24, the sea-weary eyes were gladdened
with the sight of the snowy sea gulls. Associated in
their minds, as these birds were, with the idea of
land, they brought many pleasing thoughts of home.

On April 30, they spoke the whaler, *Isabella*, of
Fair Haven, near New Bedford, Massachusetts, the
captains exchanging sundry questions. This pleasant
excitement of a passing ship whiled away an hour or
two, but there was no chance to send a letter home.

These were the days of the famous "monthly
concert of prayer for missions." It was natural then
that on Sunday, May 2, passing the island of Trini-
dad, Dr. Hepburn should write:

"We thought of our friends and the many prayers

that would be offered up for us to-day, and endeavored as far as our circumstances permitted, to meet with them to remember the heathen world before God, that they might be given to the Son for an inheritance. How should it encourage us to know that once every month God's people in all parts of the world put up united prayer for the condition of the heathen and the coming of the Messiah's kingdom. How pleasing is it, upon the lonely ocean, to be able to join our prayers with them."

On May 3 he wrote: "The North Star has sunk below the horizon. We watched it as long as we could. We have looked upon it at home. The pointers of the Great Bear are getting more and more dim and low. The Southern Cross has come into view." The days were shortening and the nights lengthening rapidly and woolen coats on the body and quilts on the bed were in order. Soon the land birds, called the "Cape hens" were flying round the vessel.

On May 12, Dr. Hepburn had to be husband, physician, nurse and friend, when a little baby son about six months old was born dead and was committed to the deep, about eight o'clock in the evening. In the narrow berth, six feet by two, in a dark room and on a rolling ship, with no mother or woman friend near, the young wife had few conveniences of any kind. The next day, a terrible storm broke. The pitching and rolling of the ship, the tossing in the berths from side to side, the water from the billows breaking on deck and coming down into the cabin, the terrible noises, the roaring of the wind among the spars and cordage, the dashing of the waves and the tumbling about of chairs and everything not lashed firmly, the creaking of masts and partitions, the cries and stamping of sailors, causing a dreadful jumble of noises, combined to make a terrible night. Yet the record is, "We did not complain, however, but felt thankful for what mercies we had, which were many."

Soon the barometer of optimism was rising. A specimen record is: "Mercy and kindness have attended us all along. Our time is spent generally very pleasantly and profitably. It seems like a continual Sabbath to us, and I trust will be a good preparation for the duties upon which we expect soon to enter. All the future is dark and unknown to us, but we can go on, committing our way unto the Lord. Happy are we, if our afflictions drive us nearer to God and that they do not harden our heart and that we can still come to him." This is the spirit of Toplady's hymn, beginning, "If, on a quiet sea," in which one stanza reproduces Hepburn's thought.

> But should the surges rise,
> And rest delay to come,
> Blest be the tempest, kind the storm,
> Which drives us nearer home.

Coleridge's "Rime of the Ancient Mariner" had either not been read by the Yankee sailors, or else had no terrors for them — although the weird poem had been in print for over fifty years — for they had no compunctions over hooking an albatross and drawing it on board. The Doctor noticed that after various other birds had fought stoutly for a piece of fat dropped in the ship's wake, making a great racket over it, the attention of the albatross was attracted. Then this majestic bird swooped down and put an end to all noise and quarreling by devouring the fat himself. If, however, there was a hook concealed in the bait, he got himself into a difficulty, which might be the prelude of his being hauled on shipboard. One of the birds caught, measured eight feet from tip to tip of the outspread wings. The body was larger than that of a goose, the eye was large and black, and the bill was about six inches long.

Notwithstanding the Doctor's medical and husbandly cares, his distressing anxiety of mind, loss of sleep and want of exercise, he kept in excellent health. He actually learned Paul's secret and began to rejoice in his disappointments. He wrote: "We find prayer to be the only means of comfort and we never enjoyed it more. The truths of the Bible are more readily apprehended and felt. We have been taught patience, dependence on God, and I trust faith, hope, love and humility have all been made to flourish through this affliction. The Lord is undoubtedly answering many of my prayers for holiness and communion with him, *but in a way I did not expect.*

(Italics in original.)   But thanks be to him for his great mercies! O for grace to improve it more, and that patience may have its perfect work!"

I have quoted thus fully from young Dr. Hepburn's journal, written over seventy years ago, since it opens a great window into his soul life. In later years, he did not put down so fully the thoughts that revealed his personal religion. His character was already formed in these early days, and he remained much the same man throughout his long life. His was a pilgrimage of serene faith, with an even temperament, so that he never wasted time in repining or in sentimentalism, but went straight ahead in steadfast work. As the Hebrew of the moving pictures in Psalm 84 would phrase it, "Passing through the valley of weeping, they make it a place of springs."

V

IN THE ISLAND WORLD OF ASIA

DURING the whole voyage the Doctor's anxiety for his wife was great. From the time her feet touched the deck, until thirteen weeks had passed, she had not one full day of comfort or good health. These were the days of old-fashioned orthodoxy in medicine and in ship's discipline. The Doctor's medicine chest showed a goodly store and use of heroic and standard remedies, and on one day a sailor was flogged for breaking into the cook's galley and stealing some meat. Then followed another terrific storm, in which the royal mainsail getting loose, the wind tore it in shreds, while the waves kept breaking over the deck, the cabin and companionway being constantly wet with the salt water. On the eighty-fifth day out, in the Indian Ocean, they passed the island of New Amsterdam — the crater of an extinct volcano, and rich in hot springs. Even a hill crest in the ocean was a welcome sight.

Not till the ninety-first day out, was the battered lady able to be out of her bunk, but on Sunday, June 13, we find this entry:

"Clara went on deck this afternoon. How thankful we should be to a kind and merciful God, who has raised her up from her sickness and restored health to her feeble body. She also sat down with them at the table. This is a day of mercy."

They now began to pack their trunks and to write their letters homeward. One day the ship sailed two hundred and twelve miles. Under date of June 16, we find in the journal Mrs. Hepburn's delicate penmanship, telling of letters already penned for home, and the addition: "My strength is daily increasing. How great is the goodness of God in raising me once more to health. O that I may serve him all the days of my life." Verily the prayers of this pioneer of the Christian education of women in Japan were answered. It was for the writer and his wife, in 1892, to exchange merry jests with her at her home in East Orange, as "Japan's first schoolmarm."

Being now within five hundred miles of North Holland island, the sailors were kept busy cleaning and scrubbing the deck and paint, preparatory to seeing land; but the trade winds were very light and variable for two days. On the ninety-ninth day, they expected to pass the forest-covered Christmas Island at night, and to descry Java Head on Wednesday. A contrast, almost laughable, was presented next day in seeing a pure-white tropic bird, sailing high in the air, rare and radiant, with the commonplace booby bird close at hand. On Wednesday, June 21, the one hundred and first day out, they made the island of Java about ten o'clock in the evening. They waited until daylight to enter the Straits of Sunda.

Then burst upon their eyes the superb beauty of this "Pearly Island of the Orient," with its mountains, clothed in verdure to the water's edge and retiring and rising one above the other. With a glass they could see the trees waving in the wind. A most delicious odor was borne by the land breeze to the ship. It was the perfume of blossoms, rather than the piquancy of spices. Two American ships lay at anchor in the New Bay. At eight in the morning, they passed Gasa Head, a bold bluff, and soon they saw a Malay *prahu* in the distance. Later on, the great Krakatoa peak, thirty miles distant, loomed up. As seen in the morning light by Dr. Hepburn, when eleven miles distant, this cloud-capped peak was robed entirely in greenery.

This is the famous volcano, whose eruptions on August 25, 27, 1883, were the most stupendous on record. They sent columns of dust and ashes in the air to the height of seventeen miles, causing darkness in the sky one hundred and fifty miles distant; making detonations that were heard more than two thousand miles away; causing sea waves that were propagated as far as the English Channel; filling the atmosphere of the old world and even America for many months with the dust that gave rise to the memorable "red sunsets" of that year; and, through tidal waves, causing the death of thirty-six thousand human beings on the shores adjacent. In 1886, Verbeck of Batavia wrote a book fully describing this amazing phenomenon. In 1841 and in 1883,

[41]

Dr. Hepburn was equally interested in this mighty landmark.

Four vessels were in sight and many Malay fishing boats were visible, when the missionaries sent their letters on board the bark *Florida*, from New York at Canton. They learned that the ship *Vespasia*, which sailed from Boston an hour later than the *Potomac*, had arrived the day before.

The island of Java, as described by Dr. Hepburn, had then a population of six million souls. Its area is fifty thousand square miles, so that it is a little larger than the Doctor's native state, or about the size of England. It is interesting to-day to compare the history and development of the two islands of Java and Cuba, so much alike as to their relation to the continent nearest to them, of much the same size, and in the same latitude.

Under Spanish rule there were probably never as many as three millions of people on the "Pearl of the Antilles," whose story was a monotonous one of misery and wretchedness, of oppression and misrule, of iron-handed cruelty and frequent rebellion, until taken hold of by the United States. Java, on the contrary, with a present population of over thirty-three million of contented and happy souls, with nearly six million domestic animals, and over seven million acres under cultivation, has been wisely governed; and its story, since the days of Hepburn, is in the main one of peace and prosperity.

The ship kept beating about all day June 25, in

SURABAYA, ON THE ISLAND OF JAVA

sight of Angere, without making much headway. Malay boats came alongside. On one of these — a family affair — were eight persons, men, women and children, all of spare habit with copper-colored complexion. The men had on pantaloons reaching down to the knees, and a jacket; the women wore only a *sarang*, or tight petticoat, and all had handkerchiefs tied over their heads, and teeth colored red by chewing the betel nut. Their lips were black, giving their mouths a very disgusting appearance.

In their cargo was a little of everything — chickens, monkeys, squirrels, paroquets, cocoanuts, pineapples, plantains, bananas, oranges, shells, yams, mats, deer horns, birds in cages, and eggs. "However ignorant of what we esteem knowledge they had all the shrewdness and ingenuity of bargain makers." The Doctor wrote: "God has made them of the same blood as ourselves. They possess the same rational and intelligent souls and are capable of being brought to a saving knowledge of Jesus Christ, to be made heirs of eternal life. Their villages will doubtless one day resound with songs of praise and prayer to the true God."

When the *Potomac* anchored off Angere, they spoke the bark *United States* from Boston, on her way back to Batavia, whence she had sailed a few days before, having sprung a leak. On this ill-fated vessel which took out a party of missionaries, the bride and groom had expected to sail, but arrived in Boston too late. Badly leaking, this ship put into a port in South America, and was detained there several months.

At five in the afternoon of June 26, as the ship cast anchor near St. Nicholas' Point, they heard the birds singing in the trees. Purchasing some cocoanuts, they found their first land drink very delightful.

These last few days, while the ship was beating her way in, against a head wind, though full of excitement, were tedious, because the two passengers had got out of their routine and ship habits. Very different from the modern promptness of a steamer, was the uncertain movement of a sailer. Nevertheless this was an era when the American flag and ships were visible in almost every sea — so different from this era of shrunken American commerce, when the Stars and Stripes, except on our national vessels, are rarely mirrored on Asiatic seas.

The Doctor's constitutional timidity broke out afresh. He wrote: "I long to be on land, and yet I tremble when I think of what is before me. The Lord only knows whether I shall be a blessing or a curse to the poor heathen, whether I shall be a faithful servant or a cumberer of the ground. There is something wrong with me, or I would not feel as I do. I cannot look up with confidence to God. A load of sin presses on my soul. O that the Saviour would help cast my burdens on him and return to him with true humility and repentance."

The Dutch were the first to show true sympathy with alien races. They founded the initial Asiatic

Society, and began the first systematic study of the deepest thing in man — religion. They were pioneers in the great work of the future, and in the special task of the twentieth century, of bridging the gulf between the Occident and the Orient and preparing the way for the subsequent union and reconciliation of the East and the West.

Before landing Dr. Hepburn wrote: "What I wish to know of the Javanese: Of what religion? What their religious ceremonies? What has been done for them by Christians? What is the policy of the government toward them and the missionaries? How many missionaries reside in the islands, and of what society, etc."

VI

IN THE DUTCH EAST INDIES

ON Monday afternoon, June 10 — the one hundred and seventh day out — when in the midst of about twenty ships, of which two were American, at four miles from the city of Batavia, the anchor was dropped and the supercargo left in the boat for land. The next day Dr. and Mrs. Hepburn left the ship in a boat pulled by four Malays. In a little over an hour they were at the head of the canal, which reached into the heart of the city. They passed four Chinese junks and in the narrow stream saw Chinese boats, in one of which sat a woman holding her god upon her lap.

Everything was new and strange, the people, their dress, language, boats and houses. The numerous Chinese in the city, — many of them quite wealthy, having more energy, industry and ingenuity than the Malays or Javanese, — were seen sitting in their shops engaged in all kinds of employment.

At the office of Mr. Darling they met Mr. Thompson, an American missionary who lived about five miles out, among the Malay dwellings. He invited them to stay with him, and they gladly accepted. Mr.

Thompson, with his wife, kept a boarding school in his house. The eleven pupils, Malay and Chinese, none of them over twelve years, were quick to learn and sang some of our tunes with great spirit and accuracy.

The natives were nearly all Mohammedans and very bigoted, being especially tenacious of their ceremonies. The missionaries had no difficulty in refuting the native arguments, but it was hard to get Javanese to accept and practice Christianity.

Although American and Dutch missionaries had been laboring for many years, and many children had been baptized, the Doctor could not hear of any adult Malay that had sincerely embraced Christianity. Yet — as throughout his life — the Doctor did not speak positively on the subject of missionary success, as his information was very limited. He always wanted facts, before making inductions. He was not a child, to plant seeds one day and get up early next morning to see them sprout, nor did he expect the baby of a week's age to talk, run, or read. He felt the force of the proverb concerning fools and their snap judgments upon unfinished work.

Batavia was really a double city, consisting of the new city and the old, the latter being very Dutch in appearance with two-storied houses whose high pointed roofs were covered with tiles. These were usually inhabited by Chinese, who were the only mechanics in the place. The Malays were generally seen employed as servants in families, as coachmen, footmen, soldiers, coolies, boatmen, farmers, etc.

The Americans and Europeans lived in the new city, which was very handsome and delightful, and in houses set some distance back from the street. They had beautiful gardens planted with trees and laid out in walks. Built of brick, covered with white stucco, and usually one story high with large verandas in front and behind, these were very tasteful and well adapted to a hot climate. In the cool of the day, doors and windows were opened. The foreigners lived in elegant style.

The Doctor wrote:

"There is indeed more luxury and elegance than is to be found in any city of America. The servants are very numerous. Every family has its carriage, and some keep as many as eight horses. This may be because of their small size, not more than four feet high, and their easily giving out on account of the heat, so that the same span of horses cannot be used except at intervals of two or three days. Houses are cheap. They may be had very good for twenty-five or thirty dollars. Early in the morning, and after four o'clock, is the only time that Europeans think it proper to expose themselves to the sun. They take a cup of coffee early, as soon as they are up; breakfast at eleven; dine at five, six, or seven, and take a cup of tea at nine or ten P.M.

"There are many canals running through the city. Batavia is indeed a beautiful place. It puts me more in mind of New Haven than any place I have seen. The vegetation is really abundant and rich. The

A NATIVE CHURCH
Dutch East Indies

cocoanut, the plantain and the orange trees and mangosteen are very common. There are several public buildings in the city, some of them handsome, and several large plains or open squares used for military parade. The Malay soldiers go barefoot. Their uniform is blue. The roads are excellent, very level, and macadamized."

On Wednesday, July 7, after a week's stay on land, the missionaries again boarded the ship. Two days later they entered the Straits of Banca. Passing the low and flat coasts of Sumatra, they crossed the equator on Sunday, July 11, and passed the island of Singin on Monday, anchoring off Singapore, the City of the Lion, that afternoon.

Singapore was then new, having been first settled in 1819. That year it had but one hundred and fifty inhabitants. In 1841, there was a population of forty thousand, and the city had an ever-increasing trade.

There were souls enough to save in this cosmopolitan city, containing sixteen thousand Chinese, and ten thousand Malays, as well as Bengalis, Hindoos, Arabs, Jews, Portuguese, Dutch, English, French and Americans. There were also Bugis, who came from the islands of Celebes, and had a language of their own, though they spoke Malay.

After leaving the ship, Dr. and Mrs. Hepburn were made comfortable by Mr. McBride. Within a few hours they met Messrs. North, Dickinson, Abeel, Stronach, Davenport, and Mr. and Mrs. Savelli. Mr. North had a mission school and Mr. McBride had a school of nine Chinese pupils. They also met Mr. Keasbury, who had a school of thirteen boys and a lithographic press. He lectured in Malay on Sunday mornings.

The missionaries held a prayer meeting, conducted by Mr. McBaylis, the Chinese teacher, in the schoolroom, which was attended also by several Chinese, most of them the missionaries' servants, and boys of the school. After hearing Mr. Abeel preach, Dr. Hepburn wrote: "He is a very affectionate, pointed, plain, practical and elegant preacher. He faces the truth in his own heart. In the afternoon, these teachers taught themselves in a mutually delightful Bible class. In the evening, Mr. Stronach preached in English, but with a good Scotch brogue."

Concluding to remain at Singapore, Dr. Hepburn renewed his study of Malay, and soon became very fond of his teacher, Abdoulla.

The first view of a native funeral was interesting, as it passed before the missionary's gate. "It seemed to be rather a disorderly procession of thirty or forty men. The body was laid in a palanquin, carried on the shoulders of four men dressed in white. The bier was hung with white and decorated with cut paper. The bearers walked on white long cloth, which was laid down for them. It was attended by a monotonous noise of beating of drums and occasional discharge of a musket. There appeared to be no solemnity or seriousness, but much anxiety to show themselves."

On September 1, the Doctor wrote: "Yesterday was one of the great days among the Chinese. The streets in their quarter were alive and crowded with people. Here and there was a table set out, groaning under the provisions with which it was loaded. Fruits of every description, fowls, also, and pork were common. Flowers and cut paper, and — in one place — a huge and hideous image was set up. This day was in honor of the disconsolate ghosts, who are supposed to partake of the food prepared for them. It is suffered to remain untouched until after nine P.M., when they all set to and devour what the ghosts leave, which is not a small part of the whole. Sometimes the provisions are placed on a high scaffold for the poor, who have a great scrabbling for it, with not a few broken shins. The Chinese, it is said, do not believe in it themselves, but merely retain the custom because it is a custom."

After such a long tossing on the ocean, the Doctor felt that it must be almost sinful to be so comfortable and happy. He wrote: "How many are the privileges we enjoy in this land of heathenism! We all have pretty good health and food and raiment. . . . We get along very comfortably — I am afraid too much so."

From the first he taught the boys singing. He found this a difficult task, for their voices were harsh and lacked fullness of tone. An additional reason for their slow improvement was their inattention. "But," added the Doctor, "this may be owing to my inability to make the study interesting." He invested some cash in Chinese idols to send home to awaken interest. There were two things Dr. Hepburn always believed. One was that interest in such an altruistic work as foreign missions — an enterprise so antipodally opposed to selfish, six per cent ideas — must be constantly stimulated and persistently nourished; and that, while teaching and preaching are such natural procedures, pupils and hearers must be attracted, or else, as is probable, the fault lies with the preacher or teacher. He was bound to be interesting and he was.

It was while at Singapore that he met Rev. Samuel Robbins Brown, "A Maker of the New Orient," and his wife, who were visiting this port for Mrs. Brown's health. This was, as he wrote, "the commencement of an intimacy of nearly forty years. How little we thought then that we should labor twenty years together in Japan."

Singapore was soon to be left for China, but not before a new link, in the chain of associations with this their first field of labor, was to be forged for the Hepburns. Here was born their first living child, a son, whose stay on earth was but a few hours. How many missionaries, all over the world, away from the homeland have had this experience! Committing, in alien soil, to the care of the Resurrection and the Life, the precious form of what they would gladly retain as the Father's gift, they have gone forward, with sad, sweet memories, to a more earnest consecration.

VII

INHOSPITABLE CHINA

WE must now glance at the educational invasion of farther Asia by the American missionary pioneers, of whom James Curtis Hepburn — who lived under twenty-four presidents and many administrations, from Madison to Taft — was one. Among the most brilliant of these four-year epochs, perhaps the most brilliant of all, as to our foreign relations, were those of Andrew Jackson and Millard Fillmore. It is certain that the action of these able rulers affected most profoundly both the nation and Dr. Hepburn's life.

Under Andrew Jackson Captain Edmund Roberts, of Portsmouth, New Hampshire, was sent out as our initial American envoy to the kingdoms of Asia. In 1832, he embarked on the U. S. man-of-war, *Peacock*, with the hope of making treaties with the states of Muscat, Siam, Annam, China and Japan. He succeeded in opening diplomatic and commercial relations with Muscat, the Mohammedan African state, and on March 30, 1833, concluded a treaty of amity and commerce with Siam, the Land of the

Free. The second paragraph of this international document is quaintly interesting.

"One original is written in Siamese, the other in English; but as the Siamese are ignorant of English and the Americans of Siamese, a Portuguese and a Chinese translation are annexed to serve as testimony to the contents of the treaty. The writing is of the same tenor and date in all the languages aforesaid. It is signed on the one part with the name of the Chau P'haya-P'hra-Klang, and sealed with the lotus flower of glass; on the other part, it is signed with the name of Edmund Roberts, and sealed with the seal containing an eagle and stars."

This treaty — guaranteeing a "perpetual peace between the United States of America and the Magnificent King of Siam" — was duly ratified and proclaimed June 24, 1837.

China was not yet open to missionary work, for Edmund Roberts died June 12, 1836, at Macao, the city then occupied by the Portuguese, and his tomb, duly inscribed, is in the Protestant cemetery. In St. John's church at Portsmouth, New Hampshire, a memorial window in his honor, reared by his loyal granddaughter, the late Mrs. John V. L. Pruyn, of Albany, commemorates his life and work. It was expected that ultimately Dr. Hepburn would be transferred to the Chinese field.

The burden of prayer in Christian hearts in these days was for the opening of the great reservoir of Chinese humanity to the everlasting gospel. The

Church was not then troubled, as she is now, with the problems of amazing success and extended development.

When China was opened, through the so-called Opium War, the Hepburns broke up their home in Singapore and took ship to Macao. They arrived June 9, 1843, and made their home with Dr. S. Wells Williams and Rev. Walter M. Lowrie. In this historic port and city, then considered Portuguese territory, they were destined to spend the summer. To the Doctor especially, Macao yielded much of interest in his hours of recreation.

As early as 1516, the Portuguese, pioneers in the Far East, visited this place, and gradually there followed envoys with presents, but the violent disposition of some of the commanders brought on quarrels and war. The Portuguese, however, came again and built churches and fortifications. Thus their settlement gradually grew in numbers and strength, but the land was never formally ceded by the Chinese. The rule of Portugal at Macao could rest absolutely only so long as it remained unchallenged by the Chinese Government.

Pope Gregory III erected Macao into an Episcopal see and at least thirteen bishops were consecrated in succession to this post. The Jesuits followed in 1585, the settlers assumed the title of the City of the Holy Name of God, and were given by the home government the same rank and privileges as those of Goa, in India. Throughout the eighteenth

century Macao prospered and even into the nineteenth century it flourished, as the outlet of trade
and the residence of many foreigners.

During the troubles of the Opium War, from 1839
to 1841, the British residents left the city for greater
security. When, by the treaty of 1842, Hong Kong
became a British possession, Macao was doomed to
decay. Various fortunes attended Macao, until in
our day the Chinese again assumed sovereignty over
the city and neighborhood.

Macao has been likened to Cadiz, in shape, because
the two cities, so far apart, strikingly resemble each
other. Three hills, between two and three hundred
feet high and connected by an irregular table-land,
upon which the town is built, constitute the seaward
portion of the peninsula. The village of Mungha,
embosomed in trees and ornamented with a pretty
temple, lying a short distance within the barrier, is
noted as the spot at which the treaty between China
and the United States was signed, in July, 1844.

The wall inclosing the oldest part of the town,
pierced with two gates, was constructed — according
to local tradition — by the Dutch prisoners of war
who were captured June 24, 1622. They had come
in a fleet of sixteen sail, to seize Macao, but were
repulsed with great loss.

In the Portuguese, Parsee, English, and the old
Protestant cemeteries of Macao, are many notable
monuments, for many illustrious men from the West
died at Macao. Among the tombs are those of Rev.

Robert Morrison, the famous pioneer in Chinese scholarship and Bible translation; of his son, J. R. Morrison, a distinguished public servant; and of Edmund Roberts, our first American envoy in Asia.

The principal spot, which every visitor is expected to visit, is Camoens Grotto, the favorite resort of the immortal poet, while in banishment here.

The charming walks, the sea bathing, the hot springs, and the legends that attach to the ruins and forts—like ivy to an oak, lending a romantic charm to the place — gave the Hepburns much to enjoy, while they waited for their final move into China proper.

They sailed to Amoy in October, 1843, to join Rev. David Abeel and Dr. W. H. Cumming, his fellow laborer in the hospital and dispensary, which the two carried on together; British soldiers occupied the place from September, 1841, to December, 1845.

Amoy has special interest because of its touch with American history. It was from this port that the tea ships of the East India Company sailed to Boston to furnish a brew of Bohea on a scale not only unknown before, when the entire cargo was dumped by the Boston "Mohawks" into the salt water of the bay, but which made a tempest in a teapot assume continental and oceanic proportions. Here, curiously enough, the Chinese word *cha* — so pronounced elsewhere — is pronounced tea.

Even before A.D. 1800, Amoy was celebrated as a

trading port and the Amoy sailors traded in India and as far as Persia, and Marco Polo mentions the name of the prefectural city not far from the port of Amoy. As early as 1544, the Portuguese were at Amoy in large numbers, but the Chinese drove them out of the port, burning thirteen of their ships and killing about four hundred and fifty of their crew. Both Dutch, English, and Portuguese traded at Amoy until 1730, when the Chinese Government centered the foreign trade at Canton, but intercourse continued irregularly, with the Spaniards and others at Amoy. In 1841, the city was captured by the British forces, and by the treaty of Nanking was opened again to foreign trade. Amoy is perhaps the most accessible for foreign ships of all Chinese ports, no pilots being necessary.

The name Amoy is the local pronunciation of Hia-mun, that is, the Gate of Hia. Many pagodas and temples, serving as landmarks, and often embowered in groves of the grouping banyan trees and very picturesquely situated, stand on the island, which is about forty-five miles in circuit. However, the nakedness of the gullied, water-worn hills, with their scanty vegetation and bleak sides, detracts greatly from the natural beauty of a city which outwardly is so easily reached, though it has poor communication with the interior.

Back of the city the mountains are covered with graves and tombs, often cut out of the solid rock. As far as the eye could reach, it seemed to the Doctor con-

凌萬順粉坊

A HEATHEN TEMPLE, CHINA

tinuous Golgotha. He was struck with the great pains and expense taken with the tombs by the wealthy, though in the city it was not uncommon to see coffins of the poor piled in stacks until they wasted into their original dust. Indeed all China, governed as it was by the dead, rather than by the living, seemed in type like the ancient Roman prisoner chained to a corpse. It seemed as if China were asking, "Who shall deliver me from the body of this death?" Protruding their unseemly forms on every side of the pathways, the tombs imparted a gloomy aspect to the surrounding scenery. Nevertheless, pleasant riding and walking were found in the hinterland, which was thickly studded with compactly built villages, which teemed with human beings, who, too often, — as I heard Dr. John Talmage say, — wasted their lives and properties in "clan fights."

Although the soil of the island, except in the small valleys, was thin and unproductive, Chinese industry had overcome the original barrenness of the ground, and fairly good crops were secured. The nakedness of the land where the hand of man had not touched it, appeared by contrast all the more shocking and shameless. Shade trees seemed to be planted only in the villages and around the temples. Though animal flesh had to be brought from the mainland, as a rule, the city markets were well supplied with meat as well as with oranges, plantain, grapefruit, pears, peaches and other fruits in season.

Probably four hundred thousand people inhabited

the one hundred and forty villages on the island. Sometimes the tremendous volume of human life had an oppressive effect upon the spirits of the missionaries. The Amoy people had the reputation of being bold, proud and domineering, but generous and hearty.

The visiting foreigners from ship, camp, or city, who wished to gratify their enjoyment of the horrible, amused themselves by going out to the execution ground, where heads were chopped off weekly. Those who would study history visited the tomb of Coxinga, the noted pirate, or rebel chief, of the seventeenth century, who destroyed the Dutch Christian settlement on the island of Formosa, one of the first — as it was the largest — Protestant missions then known in the world. Coxinga opposed the invasion of the Tartars, that is, the cavalry raid of the Manchus, who were deposed in favor of the republic, in 1912. With his piratical fleets, he terrorized the coasts, making his headquarters for many years at Amoy. His old forts, watchtowers, intrenchments, and supposed burial place were pointed out. He was commemorated in statues of colossal size, hewn out of solid granite, nearly nine feet in height, the effigy of the horse, with the curiously devised and wrought caparisons, being finely chiseled in stone. Of course, like most other Chinese monuments, these had been mutilated by the European barbarians.

About 1664, the Dutch had a trading factory here and parts of the old wall were still standing. Triumphal arches with figures of Dutchmen, sculptured on them in relief, stood near the site of the former British consulate.

During most of their time, the Hepburns resided on Kolongsu island, in the western part of the harbor, where was the foreign settlement, and which was once strongly fortified by the Chinese. Here their next child, a son, was born. This son the biographer had the pleasure of meeting in Japan in 1874. After his father's death, in 1911, he turned over the books, documents, diaries and papers, which have been used in preparing this biography.

Fresh water was plentiful because the soil was granitic. Water pipes and spouts of bamboo conveyed streams to the shore for the purpose of watering boats. In the center of the island was a singular mass of granite, in the form of immense rounded blocks, rising two hundred feet high. Many foreigners tried to scale this apex, but few succeeded in doing it. There were many ruined shrines, and the whole island seemed to be covered with graves, each headed with a tombstone and the peculiar Omega-shaped embankment so common in China.

Open to the breezes from whatever quarter, Amoy was usually a healthy place, but typhoons were rather frequent in their visitation. The foreign cemetery, which is now only too well occupied, covered about two acres in extent within a walled inclosure. Worship was held in either the clubhouse, or the consulate. Later Rev. John Alexander Stronach built a neat little chapel, and preached to the community.

Tigers were then rather frequent in the hinterland, hiding among its bowlders, and even down into our day, furnishing capital sport for the hunters with breech-loaders. The conspicuous bushy tail of the fox was much in evidence, but, except that he occasionally circumvented the noisy watch cur of the villages and made off with a fowl, he seemed to have had nothing like his European cousin's reputation for cunning. The weasel was more than rival to the fox, though in transformation stories taking the place of the wolves of our ancestors, truly believed in as changelings. This animal, of buff-colored fur and measuring eighteen inches, had a bad name for ravaging the hen roosts, but stood well with the people when he varied his diet with rats, of which there were various species, both numerous and troublesome, especially when high tide drove them out of human habitations into the open, to seek food and refuge.

Birds were plentiful, such as the kestrel, falcon, sparrow hawk, buzzard, kite, the osprey, the great and the sparrow owl, the butcher bird, or shrike, the thrush, the magpie-robin and the tailor bird. The white heron was a striking figure in the irrigated rice fields.

These were the days before the malevolent function of the Anopheles mosquito, as a disease carrier, had been suspected, and also previous to the amazir.g triumphs of science, through which military stations in the tropics have been made among the healthiest in the world. Soon after Dr. Hepburn's arrival, he found that the English soldiers were dying off numerously. Then, before many months had passed, he and his wife were down with the malarial fever.

There was no lack of congenial companionship, for this was the rallying point of that picket line of educational pioneers in Asia, who began the work whose fruits are seen to-day. In later years, in Japan, Dr. Hepburn delighted to tell about his early life at Amoy, where he was intimate with Morrison, Milne, Medhurst, Muirhead, Peter Parker, Abeel, Walter Lowrie, Bridgman and Culbertson.

The climate and the water, however, were very hard on the missionary women, and within a few months four of these died. Of the men, two were drowned, one of whom, Walter Lowrie, was captured and thrown overboard by the Chinese pirates, who long infested these waters. Yet true it is, "through the dear might of Him that walked" on Galilee,

> " They sleep as well beneath the purple waves
> As those whose graves are green."

Hoping to recuperate, the Hepburns went back to Macao for a time, but not improving, they reluctantly decided to come home and so left for New York in the ship *Panama*, Capt. Griswold, Nov. 30, 1845. After a voyage of three months and a half, they arrived in New York, March 5, 1846, just five years from the day of sailing from Boston.

VIII

THE METROPOLITAN PHYSICIAN

REFORMED Christendom recognizes the great Prussian, Karl Friedrich August Gutzlaff, as the modern "Apostle to China." In 1826, under appointment of the Netherlands Missionary Society, he went out to Java, mastered the Chinese language and entered upon a career of vast usefulness. Two years later, he moved to Singapore and then to Bangkok, where he translated the Bible into Siamese. He made various voyages along the coasts of China and Korea, and published several books on China and some in Chinese. The work, however, which links his name with Japan, was his attempt at a translation of the Gospels into the language of the far eastern archipelago, then isolated from the world.

Some of these innumerable waifs, periodically driven out to sea by storms, which, from before the days of history, strewed the Nippon islanders as seed along the shores of Asia, America and the Pacific Islands, reached Macao in Gutzlaff's time. From these Japanese sailors, uneducated and ignorant men as they were, he learned a measure of Japanese.

Forthwith, with poor tools and material, rudely, but probably for the first time in history, a complete book of the Bible was put into Japanese.

The characters used were those of the i-ro-ha (kata-kana, or square syllabary), of which there are forty-seven. The manuscript was first pasted, face downward, on blocks. Then the paper was rubbed off piecemeal with the moistened ball of the finger, leaving the ink upon the board, from which all but the black lines on the surface was cut by native workmen. This little book was printed in 1838, on the press of the American Board at Singapore.

Dr. Hepburn, on seeing this very strange text, in 1841, inquired into its history, secured a copy and with other curiosities sent it on to New York. It was duly deposited in the library at the Mission Rooms, in Centre Street, New York City, to slumber, perhaps untouched, until 1859. We shall hear of this little book again.

Gutzlaff supported himself most of the time independently of any mission board, serving for a while as interpreter and secretary of the British Legation, thus helping to bridge the gulf between Orient and Occident, or rather, between two of the most conceited peoples in the world. He practiced medicine and was greatly beloved by the Chinese. In 1844, foreigners not yet being allowed to penetrate into the interior, Gutzlaff founded a training school for native gospelers, and in four years forty-eight young Chinese were sent out to preach Christ among their countrymen.

He died in 1851, but men kindled by the message
from his lips or pen, took up his work. Verbeck of
Japan heard his living voice in the Moravian church
at Zeist in Holland and the boy's imagination was
touched. Long afterwards, when ill in Arkansas,
Gutzlaff's voice, reënforced by the Spirit of God, bade
this Americanized Dutchman arise and prepare for
that forty years of service which made his name an
indelible record in Japanese history. David Livingstone, at Blantyre, toiling at his spinning jenny in
a cotton mill, read Gutzlaff's "Appeal," and resolved
to obey his Master's call to China. The Opium War
hindered his going east, so at Moffatt's suggestion he
gave his life to Africa. How many others followed
the Master, because his servant Gutzlaff pointed the
way, may never be known on earth. The Prussian lighted a beacon in the Orient and many saw and
were glad. "Behold how much wood is kindled by
how small a fire!"

It was while Gutzlaff's messages were thrilling elect
souls in Europe that Hepburn — beaten back from
his goal, like the arctic explorer who finally compels
victory — reached New York. His first missionary
experience, lasting five years, seemed almost a total
personal loss, as well as a great disappointment. No
other opportunity for missionary usefulness presented itself, and it looked as though he must end his
life as a medical practitioner among his fellow Americans. For thirteen years, he was an active citizen
in New York, when the great city lay for the most

[66]

part south of Fourteenth Street. Nevertheless he still cherished secret hopes of returning to his chosen field.

From a very small beginning, his practice gradually improved, until it was more than sufficient for his own support. Twice he passed through epidemics of cholera and won golden opinions by his success. He made a specialty of diseases of the eye and gained notable fame as an oculist. He was always active in church work.

"When you were practicing in New York, didn't you find that you couldn't get time to go to church?" asked a physician of him once, in Yokohama.

"I had no difficulty in getting good practice in New York. There's always room at the top of the ladder," said Japan's factotum, with a mischievous look, "and I made it a point to go to church, too, and I sang in the choir. 'Where there's a will there's a way.'"

The future seemed to open to him all that a physician and a Christian layman could desire. Husband and wife were happy in their environment. Yet his household was not free from sorrow. Three children, all boys, were born to them in the New York home, but all died of scarlet fever and dysentery, at the ages of five, two, and one years, respectively. After the death of her beautiful boy, Charles, Mrs. Hepburn took charge of the class in the infant school of which her little son had been a member. So it came to pass, in God's providence, that his household being reduced to the same number as when in China, the Doctor could all the more easily move, when the call should come to go out and heal the unhealed millions of the East.

The events which led to the return to the Orient began in 1853, when the government of the United States made a more powerful impression upon the world at large than by any act done since the Declaration of Independence, in 1776. President Fillmore — not a prophet, but a man of initiative and constructive statesmanship — dispatched a fleet to Thornrose Castle in the far Pacific, under command of the brother of the hero of Lake Erie. Commodore Matthew Perry, through consummate diplomatic skill, won the Japanese to open — but only on a crack — the door of their long-sealed hermit empire. He was not successful in persuading the islanders to allow commerce and the residence of merchants or missionaries.

The honor of this great achievement was reserved for Townsend Harris, an ex-New York merchant and former president of the Board of Education in the city of New York. By patience, adroitness and skill as a diplomatist, and severe labor during many months as a teacher and enlightener, he persuaded the Yedo Government to open four ports to foreign residence and commerce. The date was fixed for July 4, 1859, when Yokohama, Nagasaki and Hakodate were to be laid out as foreign settlements, and business was to begin. Dr. Hepburn had read Commodore

Perry's "Narrative," edited by the Rev. Dr. Francis Hawks, a New York Episcopal rector, and was intensely interested. Even greater was his joy, when he read the provisions of the Harris treaty, which meant the opening of the empire to Western civilization and pure religion.

There were Christian men at that time in the waters of Japan, who took in the situation. They foresaw both the conditions, the difficulties and the promises of missionary success. One half of the triumphs — "brain-victories" the Japanese call them — over ignorance, bigotry and prejudice are won, when a frontal attack on these rocky fortifications is avoided and a well-planned rear or flank movement is made. Especially is this true if the newcomers can not only disarm would-be opponents, but can so throw the light upon the supposed phantoms and bugbears that dance as specters in the brains of unsocial hermits, as to make the bullies, the bigots and the ignoramuses ridiculous in their own eyes. Now the Japanese, almost all then, and millions of them now, know nothing about the Christianity of Jesus, having only vague and distorted notions as to what his service is. Their fancies bear as much resemblance to reality as do the visions of a nightmare-ridden man, or the victim of delirium tremens, to reality. Rural Japan is still, for the most part, frightfully pagan.

Happily, in 1859, there were three Americans who grasped the situation. By their influence and personality, they were able to guide the Christian attack upon Japanese disease, moral filth and ignorance, and to plan the educational conquest of the country. A refined Dutch gentleman, Mr. Donker Curtius, who had just signed a treaty of commerce with the Japanese, dropped the remark that gave these three men their topic of deliberation. One of this trio was Dr. S. Wells Williams, formerly interpreter for Commodore Perry, and then secretary to the American Legation in China. To-day, his fame as the author of the best book yet written in any language on China, and as printer, lexicographer, missionary, diplomatist, friend and adviser of the Chinese, and general pioneer of Christianity, civilization and Americanism in the Far East, is as steadily sure as is the shining sun. Beside him were Rev. E. W. Syle, of the American Episcopal Church, then sailors' chaplain at Shanghai, and later rector of Christ Church in Yokohama. He had married the sister of Hon. Henry Winter Davis of Maryland and was a shining instance of an Englishman reënforced with American ideas. The third man was Rev. Henry Wood, naval chaplain of the U. S. frigate *Minnesota*, and later of the *Powhatan*. At Nagasaki, six young Japanese invited him to become their instructor during his stay in port.

The Dutch, having always been friendly to the Americans, had smoothed the way for Perry both at home and at Nagasaki. King William II of the Netherlands had even personally recommended the

Japanese to open their country to the great republic; and Mr. Curtius, the Dutch consul, having talked with many Japanese officers, told Dr. Williams that they were ready to allow all possible trading privileges to foreigners, "if a way could be found to keep opium and Christianity out of the country."

In other words, if the Japanese could prevent the so-called Christian powers from forcing on them a poisonous drug that debauched human bodies and souls, and if they could keep out the dreaded "pestilential sect called Christian" — then inextricably joined, as they supposed, to political power and armed force — they would be liberal-minded on the subject of commercial intercourse.

Dr. S. Wells Williams was a profound student, both of history and of human nature. He saw at once that what the Japanese feared were foreign intervention and domestic political perils from British economics and State Churchism. In a word, the Japanese were three hundred years behind the times in their notions. They supposed that the old dogma, that the world had been divided in half by the Pope and given to Spain and Portugal, was still valid. They imagined that, in another form, the Inquisition and political interference in the affairs of the Far East were yet the ruling ideas in the West. Of the free Christianity of America and the British colonies, divorced from state control or inspection, they were absolutely ignorant.

So this scholar and historian called together his

two fellow lovers of the Master and a conference was held, probably on the deck of the *Powhatan*. They resolved, according to the Japanese proverb, to attempt the traditionally impossible, and to "disperse a fog with a fan" — that is, blow away the dense ignorance of the Japanese with letters home. Each one agreed to write to his own missionary board, urging them to be careful in their choice of the right kind of men, who should teach the Japanese what true Christianity is and win them to the true faith.

Nevertheless the watchmen of the Church had not been sleeping at their posts. In 1855, the Presbyterian Board made request of D. B. McCartee, M.D., their missionary at Ningpo, China, to visit Japan and report upon its possibilities as a soil for gospel seed. Going to Shanghai, the Doctor found it impossible to procure a passage to any Japanese port. Nor would he have been allowed to land, if he had sailed; for the Perry treaty opened no ports, except to sailors in need or in stress of weather. So the Executive Committee in New York waited until the Harris treaty opened a possible door. Then it was resolved to enter. The call, "Go ye into all the world and preach the gospel to every creature," had been ringing in the chambers of the soul of Dr. and Mrs. Hepburn. Ever ready for service, they had devoted themselves to the good of their fellows; their consuming idea was obedience to God. So Dr. Hepburn turned his back on the alluring prospect

ON THE TOKAIDO

of a continually increasing and lucrative medical practice in a metropolitan city, and—on January 6, 1859—wrote a letter to the Board offering himself and his wife for the new field. On January 12, 1859, his offer was accepted, and Dr. J. Z. Nevius —at that time in China, but ready to take service elsewhere because of the failure of the health of Mrs. Nevius—was appointed associate with him in the new enterprise. This action was as the wind of the Spirit upon the smoking flax. Instantly the candle was lighted that has steadily illuminated humanity in the Japanese archipelago to this day.

The central port opened by the Townsend Harris treaty was not Yokohama, which was then a little village of fishermen — the Strand, as the name signifies — across the bay from Kanagawa. The latter town, which was named in the treaties, lay on the great highway to Yedo, called the Tokaido. This Eastern Sea Road had received its name centuries before, when the center of civilized Japan was in Kyoto and all east of the Hakone mountains was "Adzuma," or the Broad (Wild) East. It was at Kanagawa that the consulates had established themselves, while the foreign merchants insisted on Yokohama.

Mr. Harris had argued the matter of allowing teachers and missionaries to live in Japan. In his diary of June 8, 1867, he thus summarized his point, made after eight months of negotiation: "No classes of Americans are named in the second article, so that missionaries may actually come and reside in Japan."

Both Commodore Perry and Townsend Harris were men of pronounced Christian belief. Among the polished pagans of Japan, even in this era of Taisei (1912 – +), no superstition is more prevalent, or more assiduously fostered, than the puerile notion that Christianity is an outworn system of belief, almost wholly rejected by the "scholars" and "thinking men" of the West. In the face of facts, figures and common sense, this stupid hallucination still largely possesses the willing and credulous mind of intellectual and literary as well as rustic and too often official Japan. It is certain that this notion is the source of not a few of the biggest of their blunders made in recent years.

Happily, however, the three missionary societies then in the forefront of activity, Episcopal, Reformed and Presbyterian, heard the call to Japan sent by Williams, Wood and Syle; the Presbyterians taking action first, though the Episcopal churchmen, by transferring missionaries from China, had two of them, Rev. C. M. Williams and John Liggins, first on the soil of Nippon. The Reformed Protestant (Dutch) Church followed, sending Brown and Verbeck.

When one thinks of the superb quality of the pioneers, physical, intellectual and spiritual, two of them veterans, that were sent out from America, he must feel that the Holy Spirit guided those in authority at home. Dr. Williams wrote with joy, "We had the satisfaction of seeing within a year the agents of these three societies in Shanghai." All four of those, Williams, Hepburn, Verbeck and Brown, who lived to labor in Japan longer than an average lifetime, were the peers, in intellect and culture, of the very best of their countrymen at home.

IX

JAPAN: THE LAND OF A MILLION SWORDS

ON March 29, 1859, Dr. Hepburn was made a corresponding member of the American Geographical and Statistical Society, the document notifying him being signed by Hon. John Hay. The hope was expressed that he would contribute items, letters, or memorials on subjects relating to Japan.

On April 24, 1859, Dr. and Mrs. Hepburn left New York on the sailing ship *Sancho Panza*, Capt. Hale. Samuel, their son, was sent to boarding school. The three graves in which the little children were buried were left behind.

The two passengers on the good ship were not like her namesake, the rider of Rozinante, going out to charge windmills. On the contrary, these "beginners of a better time" had a clear idea of the coming difficulties, and before these they refused to quail. They were going to the Land of a Million Swords, yet not one of these was sharp enough to scare them from their duty.

In feudal Japan, before the era of Méiji, or Enlightened Government, each one of all the samurai,

or gentlemen, wore two swords. A brace of blades
was the mark of the privileged, who paid no taxes
or tolls and lived off the labor of the toiling masses.
Against the "foreign devils," the "hairy foreigners,"
the "bearded *to-jin*," these swords were all too ready
to leap forth. Thousands of natives, who refused to
believe that the mercantile occupation of even small
lots of lands at the seaports meant anything else
than conquest, were ready to kill at sight. These
privileged wearers of weapons numbered about four
hundred and fifty thousand. With their households,
they formed "a nation within a nation" of about
two millions, in a total population of thirty millions. They were all supposed to be bound in feudal
bonds of loyalty to their barons or other lords, but
thousands of them were free lances, who had, for one
cause or another, left the service of their masters,
forming a dangerous and ever-terrorizing element.
All Japan, so long hermit, while then helpless before
foreign armies and navies, was within an armed
camp. There were in the empire about three hundred castles, with walls, towers, strong gates and
moats. Its status was that of an armed truce.

Against this sort of courage in a host with swords,
Hepburn, the Christian knight, opposed the valor of
loyalty to his Master, and the love of his fellow men.

The ship arrived at Shanghai, China, August 29.
Detained there by sickness until October 1, the Hepburns arrived at Kanagawa, October 18, 1859, just
fifteen days before their colleagues of the Reformed

(Dutch) Church in America, Rev. Samuel Robbins Brown and Mrs. Brown.

The best residence that could be found was an old temple of the Buddhists, named Jo-Butsu-Ti, which had been rejected by the Dutch consul as a stable. The Hepburns accepted it and shared it as a habitation with Dr. and Mrs. Brown, old friends who had been missionaries in China. Considerable carpenter work was necessary in order to divide up the interior space and make the ancient thatched structure habitable. When idols and dirt were removed, then began the unpacking of boxes and the transformation of the new apartments into a home. The old temple still smelled of lamp oil and the smoke of joss sticks, and had various oriental flavors and mystic odors, so that in some places abundant whitewash and considerable scrubbing were necessary to tone down the century-old deposits to suit the senses of the new tenants.

The Japanese, though a clean people, in the main, and at certain points fanatically so, were not then acquainted with the chemistry or manufacture of soap. Even yet, this necessity of person and household is called after the Latin or Portuguese name, *sapon*, which in their mouths, at least in the Yedo dialect, becomes "shabon." Well might the Japanese of to-day raise a monument to Dr. Hepburn, for he taught the meaning, the use and the manufacture of soap, which now is not only in general use, but has even become an article of export. It is certain that that part of Japan and that section of the Japanese nation within the ken of foreigners needed soap as much as they needed Christianity, while the physical condition of the people at large had probably reached its lowest depths.

"Four menservants," wrote the Doctor, "who provided their own food, agreed to serve for two dollars a month apiece, which was really high wages in Japan at that time. I paid six dollars a month rent for the temple. The Japanese used neither bread nor butter, milk nor meat. We had brought some crackers with us and these, with rice, sweet potatoes, fish and tea furnished us with very good fare. So having our physical wants supplied with a home and food, we were thankful and happy and were all the time learning to talk, first by signs and gestures, but constantly picking up words from our servants, from the carpenters, and from the many curious Japanese who came to see the strangers who had come to live amongst them.

"Did we ever get homesick? Not very badly. Everything about us was so new and so strange, and so interesting and we were so much occupied, that we had not much time to grieve over those we had left behind. More than all, we had the presence of our heavenly Father and the joy of fellowship with him, and were of good courage and hopeful."

The family altar was at once set up for the worship of God. In this delightful communion, they were joined daily by Dr. and Mrs. Brown, and often by Chaplain Wood of the U. S. S. *Powhatan*, Christian officers or men from the navy, and Christian merchants of Yokohama. Thus the old temple was turned into a house of God.

The menservants in a country where men did all domestic and household work, had to be taught everything, mainly by example; this threw a heavy burden on Mrs. Hepburn. "But they were quick to learn, very respectful and polite, going to the door with us when we went out, and meeting us with the most profound bows on their hands and knees when we returned to the house. This ceremony, however, we found to be irksome, and soon abridged it."

The Japanese were very curious, concerning everything about the missionaries, but exceedingly reticent about their own affairs. The rulers were opposed to foreigners' knowing their language or learning anything about the people of the country. All natives near them, teachers and servants, the hucksters who sold them fish and vegetables, the guard at the gates, were spies, and so were the native officers who made frequent visits. With their restless Tartar eyes, they let nothing belonging to the strangers escape their notice. Yet by and by, discovering in time what fools they were for being so suspicious, they became by degrees less burdensome in their attentions.

Many foreigners, to the number of twelve or fifteen, were murdered during the first year, and the English Legation in Yedo was attacked and some of the guards killed, while later the house of the American minister was burned and his secretary Heusken assassinated. For the better protection of the missionaries the Japanese Government built a strong and high stockade fence around the temple and placed a guard of four soldiers at the gate.

This was the era of feudalism, when servants and commoners, that is, merchants and shopkeepers, however wealthy, and mechanics and farmers, however respectable, prostrated themselves before the men of privilege and office. These latter wore two swords, dressed in silk, paid no taxes, and were usually the tyrants, and occasionally the benefactors of the people.

These samurai, or "servants of the Mikado," were — in the main — the descendants of the warriors who had anciently subdued the aborigines in the name of their chief, the Mikado, who, as they taught, had come down from heaven. From the eighth century, the military had been separated from the agricultural and working classes. Ages of routine had hardened the lines of division and deepened the gulf between them and the people at large. The samurai included within their ranks every grade of culture and character, from the consummate gentleman and noble patriot to the lewd bully and the vile ruffian. They all lived on government pensions and stipends from their feudal lords.

Swords in old Japan were everywhere in as general and disgusting evidence as were weapons among our

medieval ancestors, or "guns" upon Western cow-
boys. As novel to the American eye as is the ubiqui-
tous uniformed soldier in Europe were these relics
of an age of force.

Those samurai who were charged with the office
of government, so far as they related to foreigners,
received the special name of "Yakunin," that is,
officials. They usually wore a washbowl-shaped
lacquer hat, on which was the gilt crest of the shogun
in Yedo.

In fact, the opening of the ports to foreign commerce, which brought revenue into the coffers of the
Yedo shogun, was a cause of bitter jealousy, as the
daimios or feudal lords saw that this new political
movement, through the treaties, was likely to benefit their overlord and the centralized government
at Yedo, thus increasing the power of their tyran-
nical master. Yet this was at a time when the
whole trend of opinion and accelerating movement
of society was away from dualism (Mikado and shogun) and in the direction of national unification under
the Mikado, or Emperor. In a word Mikadoism was
the ruling idea about to rend to destruction the old
feudal structures. The clansmen, however, could
not as yet foresee that a business era and the new
economics spelled only the abolition of feudalism.
It was only gradually, that, even the most penetrating
and intellectual of the foreigners in Japan could see
just what was going on. In commercial quarters,
especially, it was long before the national movement

was discerned, or even understood, though the clash of revolution had actually come.

It was not the nakedness of the land that at first disturbed Christian people's notions of propriety, so much as the nudity of common humanity. All nature seemed beautiful, but, in spite of any tendency to liberality of opinion, Reginald Heber's classic line came often to mind:

"Where every prospect pleases and only man is vile."

In addition to beggary, foul and loathsome disease that made the image of God repulsive and disgusting, was open and public; for there were then no hospitals in Japan. Every third person was pockmarked, blindness was shockingly common, and smallpox was always endemic and frequently epidemic. Sore heads were disgustingly frequent, while consumption made frightful ravages. A deformed child was never seen. None were allowed to survive their birth. The men were, in hot summer, usually attired only in a loin cloth. Men made it a common custom to walk from the bathhouse to their home carrying their clothes on their arms. Village women took their bath in the middle of the street, as being less likely to attract attention there than anywhere else. These daily sights awoke strange and not altogether pleasant feelings in the minds of gentlemen, and especially to ladies, accustomed both to clothing and the usual upright attitude of free citizens in a republic. As for the natives, whatever was natural, seemed right.

As a rule, American women, on their first view of such vast areas of cuticle, nearly fell into nervous prostration, while the male Britishers or republicans actually felt like using boot leather, not in cruelty, but in assisting to elevate these groveling specimens of humanity and telling them to stand up, like men who lived under the Union Jack, or the Stars and Stripes.

The Japanese diet is undoubtedly wholesome. Rice, eggs, chicken and fish, then easily accessible, had many points of attraction, but the cooking flavors were peculiar and many sorts of food or native methods of preparation had to be viewed askance at first. It is true that the senses of both tasting and smelling have to be educated. In every land the liberal-minded know that it is absurd to argue as to tastes, but much also can be said about the functions of that most prominent organ of the face which, to the Japanese, seemed on aliens to be so vast, protrusive and imposing. The natives nearly fainted at the odors of our cheeses, sauerkraut and divers varieties of condiments. They were horrified at our carving at the table of rare roast beef. Not a few of the odors in our houses and about our persons were and are to them distinctly disagreeable.

Yet missionaries, as a rule, are liberal-minded and level-headed people, who seat common sense on a high throne, and soon learn to be very tolerant and charitable of personal and national peculiarities. This is ever true, notwithstanding glaring exceptions, even among veterans and usually among the fresh, green and impetuous newcomers, who have a splendid chance to do, for the first year or two, more harm than good. Yet notwithstanding all that might be said in favor of native diet, even settled down Americans usually had the feeling, after a Japanese meal, that they had not been nourished and somehow had plenty of room within. Furthermore, it was distinctly necessary to go through an education, and even painful discipline, at times, for those deeply orthodox on the subject of meat, bread and potatoes, to accustom their interior arrangement to the new pabulum. As mutton is virtually unknown in Japan, and beef was proscribed by Buddhism, the newcomers often suffered lack of the food that stands on the hoof.

As for milk, it was not only not to be had, except for old and sick people, but it was not considered lawful thus to rob the cow or her offspring. Even if the animal mother had a full udder, she decidedly objected to any human intervention for the obtaining of the lacteal fluid. When foreigners wanted milk, it required not only the presence of the calf, but a good deal of vigorous manipulation to get the desired quart or two. In time, however, educated cows, of the proper breed, were introduced, and to-day, milk and cream are common in the large towns and cities, while in the country may be seen herds of Jerseys, Alderneys, Holstein-Frisians, and other cows.

The Japanese who will uproot and keep out the bamboo scrub undergrowth, which cuts to pieces the stomachs of the ruminating animals, sheep and cows, and will educate his countrymen to live on mutton and beef and on cheese and the other products of the cow, will achieve for his people a benefit far surpassing those of the warriors whose breasts glitter with decorations.

Sweet or "Satsuma" potatoes were common and were the delicacies of the vulgar, their use being tabooed as a rule by the highest classes. But white, or "Java" potatoes were like angels' visits in the settlements, "short and far between." For many months, Mrs. Hepburn had to depend upon ship's rations and get her meat, bread and potatoes, from the floating larders.

A missionary's daughter wrote in after years of her memories of the Hepburns' home in Kanagawa:

"If the friends, the pupils, the parishioners, the patients and the mere admirers of Dr. Hepburn could each bring but one flower as a symbol of their regard for him, their indebtedness to him and their love for him, his house would not be big enough to hold the fragrant blossoms. Do you accuse me of prejudice? Then look through my spectacles.

"Imagine, at the close of our American Civil War, in newly opened Japan, a Buddhist temple, looking like a one-story bungalow, propped on stilts, well set back from the street, in the town of Kanagawa; for Yokohama was then a mere strip of fishing smacks in the midst of a marsh. Kanagawa was a port of the country ruled, as report said, by two kings. In the large temple yard no untidy blade of grass, which struggled up, was permitted to remain. That is not *comme il faut* in a Japanese temple yard.

"A splendid maidenhair tree stood near the gate of the compound and the sunbeams sifted through the leaves upon the stalwart guardsmen who often sat at its base. A guardhouse was at the gate, and no one entered the inclosure without passing a rigid inspection. The foreigners within the temple never set foot outside of the compound, unless accompanied by a guard, which the Yedo Government had sent to protect the 'foreign devils' from any harm at the hands of fanatical natives. According to common rumor these guards also made most excellent spies. This was the dwelling of Dr. and Mrs. Hepburn, and into their temple home, they received as bride and groom my father and mother. Later on, the Doctor ushered me into the world, and from this early acquaintance down the years, with smiles and tears, is it a wonder that a remembrance of the soft kiss of the Doctor's lips and the sweet tones of his voice touch the strings of memory's harp to tender strains? When I was a child, he brought me a locket from China. When I was married and he thought I needed a scolding (not for marrying), he traveled to Tokyo to administer it. This interest, in so old a man as he had then become, was so touching that I agreed most meekly with every word he uttered, though I knew I had not deserved it."

X

KANAGAWA: PIONEER OF SCIENCE AND EDUCATION

THE first element of success in life is to know what things are first. The primal business of a missionary is to study efficiency and to raise this to the highest point.

In one of the issues of "The Korea Mission Field," in 1913, a famous but anonymous veteran, speaking from experience, under the heading, "Were I a missionary," writes:

"I would do first things first. I would soon find out that the first of first things is language study: that the Board had not sent me as the mission's councilor — I should not waste energy in trying to correct all that I thought wrong in missionary methods; that the greatest asset of a missionary's life is the gift of the Holy Spirit and the second is a mastery of the language."

What this wise son of experience says of the missionary might well apply in part at least to the *yatoi*. Many of these hired servants of the Japanese Government, on their first arrival on the soil, and often for months after that august event — so great in their

[88]

eyes — were as fresh as green persimmons. Dr.
Hepburn was, however, on his arrival in Japan,
already a seasoned veteran, forty-four years old.
He began at once to wrestle with the language.

As soon as possible, however, this army crusader,
armed with the lancet, attempted to begin medical
work. He rented a Buddhist temple, not far from
his dwelling, fitted it up, and opened it for the benefit
of submerged humanity. Soon it was thronged with
sick people of every kind, often from six to eight score
a day. Thereupon that mysterious entity, called
"the government" interfered, drove the sick people
away, shut the gate, stationed a guard before it and
allowed none to enter.

"I complained to Mr. Harris, the United States
consul and minister," wrote the Doctor, "but could
get no assistance from him, being told that the treaty
with Japan was not made for missionaries, only for
merchants. The real reason for the close of my
hospital was, I think, the desire to drive us, as well
as all other foreigners, away from Kanagawa to
Yokohama, where we would be more under govern-
mental control and could be more easily guarded" —
from native assassins and incendiaries.

The Doctor was undoubtedly right in his surmise,
as events showed. However, he was not to be
baffled in his efforts to do good, while thousands
suffered in pain, or literally rotted through neglect.
Japan was then at her lowest in physical degeneration
and disease; it is the indictment of history against

the Yedo regime of Tokugawas (from 1604 to 1868)
that they did little or nothing for the soil or the
people. Nothing could frighten the good physician,
whether by night or day, from ministering to the
suffering. Count T. Hayashi, late envoy to Great
Britain, wrote me:

"At Kanagawa, many were the accidents which
happened in the turbulent times of anti-foreign
agitation, but I was assured by the people of Kanagawa, whom Dr. Hepburn befriended, that he had
never flinched from visiting his patients, or those
people who required his help. In places that were
considered among the most dangerous, whenever and
wherever his sense of duty or the nature of his
mission called upon him to go, he went."

One of these "accidents" resulted in the death of
an Englishman and the subsequent bombardment
of the capital of Satsuma by a British squadron.
The foreigners visiting Japan, who had been accustomed to the weak and unresisting Chinese, found a
different temper among the islanders. On September
14, 1862, a party of three English gentlemen and a
lady were riding on the Tokaido, when they met the
train of horsemen belonging to the baron of Satsuma,
who, with his knights, was then bitterly angry because of a rebuff received in Yedo. While spoiling
for a fight, an altercation ensued, swords flashed
from their sheaths, and the three foreign gentlemen
were wounded, Mr. Richardson mortally. The lady,
bespattered with blood, escaped and brought the

FIRST RESIDENCE OF AMERICAN MISSIONARIES
Dr. Hepburn's Home for four years.— Kanagawa

news. The story has been told a thousand times, but it is here recalled, because Dr. Hepburn was summoned to dress the wounds of the unfortunate men. The Yedo Government was powerless to punish Satsuma, its most distant and hostile feudatory, so the British fleet inflicted punishment next year and an indemnity was paid. That taste of war was as good medicine and Satsuma became the leader in Mikadoism and unified Japan. Dr. Hepburn was called to be the pioneer of education, as well as of modern science and of the healing art in eastern Japan. As early as 1861, nine lads of rank were sent to Kanagawa for six months or so, to study English under him. As he wrote later:

"In 1861–62, the Yedo Government sent some of their best young men for me to instruct in Western knowledge and science, through the English language. My relations with these young men were extremely pleasant. Owing to the intestine troubles and impending fall of the shogun's government, the young men were recalled, some of them to lose their lives in the civil war and others to occupy high offices of honor and trust under the new government."

As a newcomer, Dr. Hepburn was obliged to attack the language single-handed, for no phrase-books, grammars or dictionaries existed. Pantomime, gesture, pointing to objects to obtain their names and to build up a working vocabulary, were the first methods. In time, a future tense was discovered. How to modify assertions was a problem. To find an equivalent for "but," "nevertheless," "notwith-standing" or "however," and for other dubitatives was a problem. The word *keredomo* was fearfully overworked, as much so as is the word "already" by a Dutchman talking English. Dr. S. Wells Williams, interpreter for Commodore Perry, was remembered as *Keredomo San* (Mr. Keredomo, or Sir Nevertheless).

Personally, the biographer never understood what the Scripture meant, which speaks of "leaping over a wall," until he tackled the Japanese language. Having had some trial of Latin and Greek, French and German in college days, and of Hebrew and Holland Dutch later, he possessed some notions of the growth and construction of language and how speech was used in the mouths of living persons, as well as formulated in books. Here in Japan, however, was a tongue that was totally different in its genius from anything either in the Aryan or Semitic family of languages.

It is true that the Jesuit missionaries from Portugal and Spain had, in the sixteenth century, endeavored to make grammars of Japanese. Their procedure was in accordance with the analogy of the tongues of southern Europe. Yet before A.D. 1600 even the modern Romance languages had not been well mastered by grammarians. Having only the Latin apparatus of thought, these Jesuit scholars had laid the speech of Nippon upon the Procrustean bed of the classics and had attempted thus to explain its peculiarities by the Latin case and verb systems. In the *wa, ni, wo, te,* and other terminations, there

[92]

did seem to be some superficial analogy, but to students in the nineteenth century — the great century of linguistic penetration and achievement — such a method was soon seen to be worse than useless.

The lack of teachers was all the more serious hindrance because natives were without the modern critical mind. Moreover, knowing their own language only as a child knows breath and a fish feels water, the first native instructors available were little better than pump stocks, from which information was extracted only after severe labor. Dr. Hepburn was very much like the prince before Thornrose Castle. He went at the language with next to nothing, but soon had leaped over the wall and was in the strange world of Japanese thought and roaming in the garden of Japanese literature.

Having already had a grounding in Chinese, he was able, after acquiring momentum, to make rapid headway in what, from the native scholar's point of view, was the best literature of Japan. The first thing to know wisely was history, for this stands first in importance of the categories, over twenty in number, of the national literature. At that time, the Nihon Guai Shi, or the official (and therefore more critical and vastly more valuable) history of Japan, by Rai Sanyo, completed in 1822, was in every scholar's hands. It had already become the chief factor in forming the political opinions of most Japanese gentlemen of alert mind. This book, more than any other, helped to create the public sentiment which ushered in the new political world of 1868, when dual government, and later feudalism were abolished and all power centralized in the Mikado. This remarkable work is written in excellent Chinese, which is the Latin of the educated native of Japan, and in its composition the author spent over twenty years of unintermitted activity.

Dr. Hepburn also read much in the classic histories of Japan, composed in Chinese, and those in the mixed script of ideographs and the native syllabary. Yet, living in a commercial seaport, he was, like most of those around him, slow to realize the force and depth of the currents of the political opinion (Mikadoism) which Rai Sanyo and the Mito scholars had started and which, after the Harris treaty, rose to a flood. Yet he knew the two different worlds of mind and social condition in Japan, and that there was a nation inside of a nation, that is, the samurai and the commoners. Vocabulary, customs and dress, as well as edicts had so divided them that a great abyss lay between. It was quite possible for educated native gentlemen to converse together for hours, in the presence of their servants or the merchant class, or farmers, without being understood or divulging secrets which they wished to keep.

There were many cases, sometimes quite ludicrous, when even at the dinner table, the learned Europeans in the legations, accustomed to deal with the higher classes only, were unable to make themselves understood to the waiters. In one instance, the most famous of all English masters of written Japanese was at an official dinner, and wished to have powdered, instead of lump sugar, on his strawberries. Using the polite term to the servant, instead of the usual alert obedience, he was met with a blank stare, followed by a puzzled look. However, sitting next to the savant was a missionary who knew the common people's talk, and making use of the vulgar term *sna sato*, that is, "sand sugar," he secured instant forthcoming of the sweet substance.

I was myself mightily amused once, when, standing with Dr. Hepburn in one of the high rooms of a tower, or "arrow arsenal," overlooking the ramparts and moats of the castle of Tokyo, I found I could help out the lexicographer. Personally, I was reminded in doing so of Landseer's picture of "Dignity and Impudence." He had tried several times to get from a group of soldiers, standing nearby, an explanation of something down below, which he wished to know about. These sons of Mars, being from an interior province, imagining that the foreigner was talking in an alien tongue, were polite but reticent. So turning to me, the Doctor asked for help in idioms of the vernacular. With the feeling of a baby playing with a giant, I put the question to the soldiers in a dialect most familiar to me and to them, and received so prompt an explanation that both the Tokyo and the Yokohama *to-jin* had a good laugh together.

Summing up, the Doctor wrote in later life:

[95]

"The Japanese written language is expressed in forty-seven syllables, each sign being composed of a consonant and a vowel, with only one final *n*, used in writing Chinese words, or to express the future tense. The method of transliterating foreign words is a very tiresome as well as inadequate one. Japanese words are not modified by gender, number or case, and have no capital letters. There is no careful system of punctuation, nor any relative pronoun, but there is a variety of personal pronouns to suit the rank or social condition of the person addressed.

"Other difficulties come from the absence in the language of terms to express the moral and immoral, the various precious stones, and the distinctive fauna and flora of Palestine. In these cases we found the Chinese written language a mine of wealth."

Compare this with the gross flattery of tuft hunters with the Japanese, who would make out the speech of Nippon to be the very quintessence of things ideally linguistic, ethical and delightful.

First impressions seem to have been the last also. In 1895, Dr. Hepburn wrote out for me an auto-biographical sketch. He said:

"The Japanese, like all other nations, have their peculiar characteristics and a national type. They differ from the Chinese and other Asiatic peoples even more than the nations of Europe differ from each other. . . . They are smaller in stature than the Chinese, quick to imitate and borrow from other nations, but often improving upon the thing borrowed and they are ready to adopt whatever they find useful to themselves. They are fickle, volatile, emotional, fond of pleasure, inquisitive, ambitious, naturally courteous and civil, intensely patriotic, brave and revengeful, desirous of standing well in the opinion of foreign nations. In morals, they are like all pagan peoples, untruthful, licentious and unreliable."

It is only fair to say that the Doctor, lover of truth as he was, had come in contact with thousands and tens of thousands of the lower classes and with but hundreds of the samurai.

The Japanese, any more than other sinful mortals, may not enjoy it thus to have their best friend hold up the mirror to nature, but then the remedy is at hand. Conversion to holiness, and not mere reformation, is what they and we need. So long as Japanese have no belief in moral accountability to God, here and hereafter, so long will they be pagans, despite all their outward polish. No jeweled decorations on the breast, or eminence or fame as soldiers, sailors or inventors can change this fundamental fact.

Furthermore, the Doctor was, in his theology — that is, in his philosophy of the facts of God and man — a Calvinist. Now Calvinism knows nothing about kings, emperors, Sons of Heaven, popes, cardinals, generals, beggars, the poor or the rich, the learned or the ignorant; but only sinners in need of salvation. No other form of faith could give him such constant assurance of the love of the heavenly

Father, and the certainty that all things work together for good to them that love him.

Calvinism is like a stained-glass window. To those outside, who can see only its unillumined and uninviting framework, set in gray and forbidding walls, it is dark and repulsive. To those inside — enraptured with the splendors of the Creator's universe — it brings all heaven before one's eyes and dissolves the soul in ecstasies. Not even Milton, in his seraphic verse, could transcend the facts in the joy of this Christ-filled man, whose inner life was a Hallelujah.

XI

AT YOKOHAMA. A MASTER OF SYSTEM

THE Hepburns lived at Kanagawa for four years, from 1859 to 1863. Then they moved to Yokohama. From the first, the foreign merchants found Yokohama across the bay so much freer from molestation and so much better fitted for trade and residence, that in spite of all official protests and to the great disappointment of Mr. Harris, they made that the center of active operations, while Kanagawa sank into the reputation of a mere suburb. Dr. Hepburn, who had assisted to survey and lay out the settlement at Yokohama, purchased a lot near "the creek," not far from a bridge which crossed the water dividing the old village from Homura. On this lot, facing what was to be Main Street, he built a house, one story high, with an attic. A house like this was desirable, for Japan is a country of earthquakes.

My own first experience of these ague fits of Mother Earth was in Dr. Hepburn's house. Early in 1871, I was sitting at his hospitable board, along with Mrs. Hepburn and Rev. Young J. Allen of China, then in the prime of his strength and power. Like myself, he was utterly unused to such strange behavior of the earth. I had just recovered from the shock of being bossed by the Doctor's Japanese servant, who imagined that I had not been properly brought up, because I took from the castor held in his hand, a drop or two of vinegar for my soup, instead of something else he thought I ought to take. Having the Hepburns as his supreme model, and being only a creature of tradition and routine, he seemed to think my behavior shocking in the extreme. We had got past the fish and were attacking the curried chicken and rice, when, as it seemed to me, the whole upper works of the house had broken loose — somewhere above my head. In a second more, I imagined that a cart loaded with bricks and drawn by a team of four horses hitched to it, was running away, and racing over the upper floors. I looked out the window, only to see the trees shaken in a way that reminded me of a terrier doing business with a rat. Yet there was not a breath of air stirring. The pictures on the wall began to sway outward and then bang against the wall paper, and the doors to open and shut, in the most uncanny way, while the windows rattled, as if ghostly personages were entering or departing. Mr. Allen jumped up to see what was going on above, or beneath, but one quiet word from the Doctor, "Earthquake," assured me that all was right. If he could sit still, when the old, settled-down Mother Earth was thus misbehaving, I could also, and I did.

Nevertheless, for some time afterwards, when in

DR. HEPBURN'S HOUSE

Yokohama

Tokyo, I labored under the not altogether groundless fear that I should wake up some night and find the chimney in bed with me. The Doctor was so far in harmony with his environment as to have no plaster on the walls, and when I looked for a smoke exit, I found only an ugly stovepipe projecting under the gable.

In this modest house, the Hepburns lived for many years, and here, many a time afterwards, I came, seeing the Doctor in his study room surrounded by books and manuscripts and with his ever-faithful translators and assistants. I met, at one time, Mr. Tahahashi Goro, the scholar who has translated also a large part of the Roman Catholic version of the Scriptures; and at another, Okuno, afterwards the church elder, poet and scholar; and, in one case, a young man destined to be the ambassador of Japan to the Court of St. James, Mr., now Count, T. Hayashi.

The Japanese, that is, the Yedo Government, were very suspicious of the missionaries at first, often sending spies to see what they were doing and what they had in their houses. Altruism might be conceivable to an islander, but how it could ever possibly exist in the breasts of men seven thousand miles away, who could spend their money and have sufficient interest in distant humanity to send out healers and helpers, was at that time unthinkable to the average Japanese. Under all designs and pretexts, was supposed to be a desire to conquer Japan and use her people only for selfish purposes. For many years this was the attitude of almost all Japanese, though later they all made glad confessions of their blindness and former inability to understand that benevolence might exist in an American heart.

By the year 1871, much light had dawned. When the ambassadors representing the Emperor came to New York, they inquired whether certain elderly ladies were living, who in 1866, at New Brunswick, New Jersey, had shown kindness (including financial assistance, temporarily) to the first two Japanese lads who had come to study in America. The eminent men took occasion to confess gladly that these and other proofs of the kindly feeling of Americans toward Japanese and the courteous treatment of their young countrymen had done more — to use the words of Iwakura and Okubo, "to cement the friendly relations of the two countries than all other influences combined."

Because the missionaries were regarded as strange folk and at first utterly unclassifiable, the educated natives feared to render any scholarly assistance to these strange men who, though in Japan far away from home, did not buy or sell. It was five months before Dr. Hepburn in Kanagawa was able to get a teacher, and afterwards he had reason to think that this person was a government spy. Moreover, despite the appalling needs of the poor and diseased, the Yedo Government at first hindered and then stopped the Doctor's benevolent work entirely, by forbidding the sick to come to the dispensary.

Thus, shut off from one field of labor, he gave himself up wholly to the study of the language and later to compiling his great dictionary.

On moving to Yokohama, however, he reopened his dispensary and was at work in it every week day, until 1879, ministering to the diseased. Finally it was closed on account of ill health. He prescribed for from six to ten thousand patients yearly, and had about him a corps of five to ten young men anxious to learn the healing art. He maintained also a medical class of young men whom he instructed three days a week, besides teaching a Bible class on Sunday. During the last five years of his ministrations in the dispensary, before commencing medical work, he gave the patients assembled every day a talk upon some Christian truth. He purposely abstained from treating foreign patients, lest he might be thought to be earning private revenue; but at times there was no other foreign physician, and he was obliged to listen to the calls of humanity; this he did gladly. During one year there was no clergyman in Yokohama, except the English chaplain, so that for those who did not attend the English Church, he had to conduct worship on Sunday.

In those days native foreigner-haters abounded and the *ro-nin* was in the land. Because of his activity, Dr. Hepburn's toils were increased. The *ro-nin*, or wave-man, was a gentleman, so called, of the samurai class, and therefore allowed to wear two swords; but he was not in the service of any one of the feudal lords, as was almost every one of the samurai, having detached himself therefrom, or having been discharged through fault. Being a free lance, he was apt to become a terror to the community. Some of the *ro-nin*, indeed, were men of the highest character, who had given up salary and support as feudal retainers, in order to devote themselves to scholarship, or some other form of honorable toil, to altruistic labors, or to accomplish purposes not easily secured when bound to a master. For the most part, however, the *ro-nin* were either violent and fanatical patriots, common drunkards, or unmitigated scoundrels, of whom the world was too worthy.

Ordinarily among gentlemen, swords did not easily leave their scabbards, for the rules governing the privilege of wearing them were very rigid, but among the lower grades of samurai, frequenters of brothels and wine shops, the sword came out only too easily. Life was held very cheap by and among these swashbucklers, and cheaper yet was the saké, or liquor brewed and sometimes distilled from rice, with the fusel oil still in it. The low price of this brain-poisoner had attracted the attention of Commodore Perry, who in a long life spent among sailors, knew its degrading effects only too well.

At both Kanagawa and Yokohama the government had built a high palisade fence, and maintained a strict guard at the gates. All suspicious characters were challenged and every native who came in or out of the foreign settlement must be known. In spite

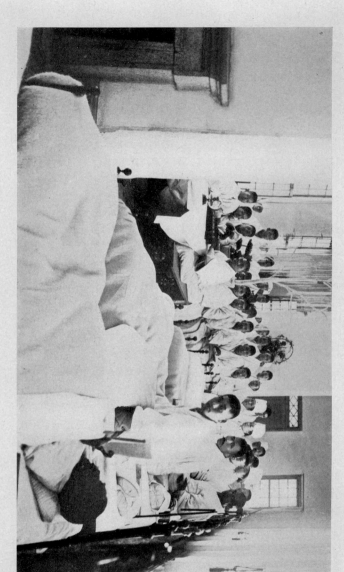

IN A JAPANESE NAVAL HOSPITAL

of this, however, not a few Russians, Dutchmen, Englishmen and others were murdered. Nearly every treaty nation contributed victims to the murderous *ro-nin*. It was not uncommon to find limbs, or hands, sheared off by the assassin's sword lying on the roads. The foreign cemetery at Yokohama tells to the old-timer some wonderful stories. Almost all foreigners, when on the highways or rambling within the seven league radius allowed them by treaty, went armed. Outside the settlement they were usually accompanied by guards for protection.

Soon after his arrival, the Doctor had found strange men near his house, who afterwards confessed that they had come to assassinate him, or to kill any other foreigner who seemed to offer easy prey. Another fellow actually took employment for the express purpose of murdering him, but after a few weeks, finding out what kind of people the missionaries were, and beholding himself as an arrant fool, he abandoned his plan. It was indeed enough to disarm the prejudices even of a demon to see this American at work every morning in his dispensary.

The Japan of our day is a land that leads the world in military and public hygiene and in successful surgery, while all the records of war, in saving the lives of the wounded, have been broken by a nation that knows to perfection the fine art of profiting by the experience and abilities of other peoples, but is largely so because of Dr. Hepburn and men like him.

Japanese freshmen, who now sneer at the mission-aries and boast of their country's progress, wonder, perhaps, whether those of us who tell of things that we saw with our own eyes, are not "blowing a big conch," are jaundiced by race prejudice, or are dealing with fiction. Indeed, it is nearly impossible for a native born in more recent years to realize the wretchedness of the million or more of the diseased, the outcast, or the beggars of the Japan of 1870.

I saw thousands of these mutilated, blind, scabby and foul creatures, who swarmed upon the public roads, begging piteously for food or for help, and bear witness to their degraded existence on the high-roads of the empire, both in the far interior and in the Doctor's dispensary. In a room able to hold about a hundred persons, there were gathered daily from twenty to seventy-five persons, of all ages and sexes, most of them foul and repulsive. Without fuss or visible emotion, though with real sympathy and profound pity, the missionary physician did his work of relief. Near or around him were from five to ten native youth, most of whom have since made their record, as men with the letters M.D. after their names. These were preparing medicine, bandages, or dressings, assisting in surgery, or in preparation of the patients. They helped the Doctor, in one way or another, while themselves learning. In the com-pany, waiting their turn, were human beings of every condition who showed the marks of sin, ignorance, misery, accident, or infection.

Here was an old man hoping for relief from some chronic disease, and perhaps only too ready to show the limb or organ that needed the attention of science or skill. Here were mothers, holding up their sick babies to the Doctor, pleading for one ray of hope. The eyes, it might be, of the little ones were eaten out with smallpox, or even a worse disease, while the maternal eyes were "homes of silent prayer." I can never forget those piercing looks into the Doctor's face. Frequently their piteous glances or importunate petitions were of no avail. Disease had gone too far, and often death was prompt and merciful. Happy indeed was the Doctor himself, when, by a pinch of powder, a bolus, a lotion, a salve, a dressing, or a surgical operation, he could bring joy and hope. Many of his most successful operations had been previously unknown in Japan.

One need not go into too much detail concerning what was at first a chamber of horrors, in which every sense was offended, but which became for the majority a place of delight. Around the walls were comforting passages from the Book of books, rich promises, words of hope and tender consolation, messages from the Great Physician.

With the help of interpreters, even in earlier years, the waiting time and fruitful opportunity made this room often the very gate of heaven to souls, whose ransom from the power of guilt, suffering and darkness began here. Yes, that dispensary was a Bethel to many of the Japanese. Dr. Hepburn's problems were not geographical, ethnic, or philosophical, but immediate and human.

Intensely human himself, out of his heart flowed streams of sympathy, help and healing. To both natives and alien dwellers upon the soil, he and his wife made their home one of abounding hospitality. All who came under his roof — whether they were lovers beginning their life voyage, or lovers long mated during years of mutual burden bearing, inquirers or visitors, scholars or common people, children or the aged, friends of missions, or their critics and enemies — felt the power of sympathy, sometimes given merely by look or word, sometimes by the application of science and skill. Benevolence had no enemies.

Whether for individuals or the nations, Hepburn's work in quality was that of a master. In quantity, when one remembers that frail body, it seems astounding. It is no exaggeration to say that for the Japanese born since 1870, he, under God, made theirs a different world to live in. Physician, lexicographer, translator of the Bible, friend of beggars and emperors, and — oh, noble task! — conciliator of missionary and merchant, he was always referred to in Japan as "Kun-shi," the righteous and noble gentleman.

In one respect, his work and personality were unique. As a rule, missionaries and merchants — the trading and the altruistic class — do not lavish much love upon each other, when they are away from home and in the presence of the heathen. The

A MASTER OF SYSTEM

men of the mart and counter, and the men of the Church and pulpit, survey humanity from such different angles, and are themselves usually such subjective victims of their own professions, notions, or environment, that mutual respect is difficult to maintain. The general attitude, on both sides, is one of armed neutrality, of icy indifference, or of amused toleration.

Happily for the first missionary pioneers in Japan, who were men of broad culture and knowledge of the world East and West, such alienation of view was not, in the sixties, at all marked, or was at a minimum; while in the case of the physician and the average human being, there was really very little of aloofness on either side. Then it was Dr. Hepburn's delight to cultivate those graces which bring out the best side of human nature. Hence from the first, he won the regard and often the warm friendship of men of every class and profession. In this way, he helped powerfully the coming of the kingdom which is not of this world.

When compelled by the government to go to Yokohama, the Hepburns were not only in danger from the *ro-nin* assassins, but from the fanatical followers of the Mikado. On one occasion, early in May, 1862, rumors reached them that Yokohama was to be attacked in force by the *ro-nins*. Upon this, their servants all decamped. Thus left alone, they packed their clothes and portable valuables and stored them in a convenient place near the pier.

[109]

Then, day and night (they dared not go to bed) until May 31 they awaited the signal agreed upon for speedy flight to take refuge on the U. S. S. *Wyoming*, one of the foreign ships lying at anchor in the harbor.

However, the order to attack Yokohama was countermanded, for the valiant foreigner-haters, despite their fanatical courage, concluded that discretion was the better part of valor. So the fiery but foolish patriots, after finding that the foreigner had teeth that would bite, let Yokohama alone and many of them actually began cultivating the soil and their hands, as well as brains. In a few years, a million swords became vulgar hardware for the field and kitchen or were stored as curiosities in museums. The Doctor lived to see Isaiah's prophecy measurably fulfilled in the Land Ruled by Slender Swords.

XII

"A GOOD WIFE IS OF THE LORD"

WHATEVER may have been "the reveries of a bachelor" in his younger days, the newly fledged physician, J. C. Hepburn, M.D., besought of his Father in heaven the gift of a good wife. He was thoroughly orthodox in his belief that a man's best fellow and helpmeet is of the Lord. Happily and fully, his prayer was answered. He received into his bosom a divine measure of blessing pressed down and running over.

In all the manifold variety of his great work in many lands, he was mightily helped by his partner, whose marital love and service lasted over sixty-five years. It is very difficult for the biographer to put down in cold blood what Mrs. Hepburn was as host, friend and presiding spirit in the parlor, sitting room, at the table in her own home, and in the social life of Yokohama, during the sixties and seventies. In those days, when American ladies in Eastern lands were few and far between, she was often spoken of on our warships, in grateful merriment, as "the Mother of the United States Navy." Many a young officer was saved from folly, impurity and dissipation by her kindly warning or helpful words. In the new settlement, she was Dorcas, Martha and Mary in one. Not a few homesick and heartbroken men and women were by her set forward in life with new songs in their hearts. What the new lighthouses on the headlands of modern Japan are to the ships at sea, Mrs. Hepburn was to many of the numerous waifs, too often wrecks of humanity, stranded in the seaport.

Most of the Japanese who came to do business with the foreigners in the sixties were hardly of prepossessing appearance, or winsome character. Indeed much of the unjust stigma of dishonesty and the suspicions, both just and unfounded, that linger among us concerning the Japanese traders, is an inheritance from this time, when the merchant of Nippon had no social standing, and trade was beneath the contempt of the native gentleman, and when possibly a majority of the native shopkeepers knew little and cared less for the high ideals of commercial integrity, which thousands of Japanese of to-day share with the best men of Christendom. Yet the testimony of many witnesses shows that the lives of not a few of these persons were remade under the influence of the Hepburns, who loved the sinners while hating their sin.

Perhaps the greatest tribute that can be paid to Mrs. Hepburn is that she was the pioneer of woman's education in Japan. To us it seems perfectly absurd that the Japanese Government in dispensing its honors, posthumous and otherwise, and bestowing

CHINESE GIRLS OF UPPER CLASS STUDYING IN JAPAN (1908)

its decorations, has so consistently ignored the part which American and other foreign women have played in the intellectual and social development of the nation, as well as through its own womanhood. One would heartily enjoy listening, with the understanding, in a session of the judges who award the marks of imperial favor, to the advocates, and also to the *advocatus diaboli*. He might thus learn what appraisal is put upon labors that re-create nations by the processes akin to leaven and sunbeams, as compared with those that suggest typhoons and tidal waves. It is certain that Mrs. Hepburn, in the eyes of the undecorated, was the beginner of woman's education in the Mikado's empire.

In 1863, at the earnest request of a Japanese physician, who wished an education for his granddaughter, Mrs. Hepburn began a school for girls. At this time education for women was not thought of in Japan. "A stupid woman is less troublesome in the family than one that is wise" is a sentiment attributed to Confucius. Those who wrote, or revised, the Imperial Rescript, in 1871, allowed even the Emperor of Japan to say, "Japanese women are without understanding." Mrs. Hepburn's school was "the mustard seed of woman's education in Japan." As was said by an eminent Japanese of character, "the first recognition by the government of the education of the nation's daughters was when a pupil of Mrs. Hepburn was appointed to assist Miss M. C. Griffis in the first school for girls in

Tokyo." Within twenty-five years from the beginning of Mrs. Hepburn's class, a million and a half of girls were under school instruction. In the words of the Emperor's immortal Rescript on Education, issued in 1890, the goal was: "No village with an ignorant family and no family with an ignorant member."

Though Providence had denied lengthened life to the Hepburns' children — all boys — except to their son Samuel, there were not wanting babies in their home, from time to time. Little Japanese waifs for one reason or another were housed and in various ways assisted on their way to adult life. The first acquaintance made by the Japanese with the peculiarities of steam, the new child born of fire and water, often resulted in disaster. On a little steamer plying between Tokyo and Yokohama, a young Presbyterian missionary and his wife lost their lives, but their babe and its Japanese *ama*, or nurse, were blown into the water, and were saved. Except for some scalds, the boy was unhurt. Where could the waif go but under the Doctor's hospitable roof? Mrs. Hepburn mothered the infant until sent to America. After leaving his parents' quiet tomb in the Yokohama cemetery, the boy grew to stalwart manhood.

Mrs. Hepburn welcomed under her roof and to her table a great many visitors. They were of all sorts, and some of them certainly not angels entertained unawares. The cloven hoof and barbed tail were better emblems of certain others. We old residents

[114]

of Japan, in Tokyo, who imitated the good example of hospitality set by the Hepburns, mightily enjoyed the fun which these freshmen and freshwomen furnished us, though the scribblers who stayed forty-eight hours on the soil and then wrote magazine articles, or made books on Japan, supplied even more merriment.

For the sting, which some of their abominable effusions must leave, ample revenge was taken by those least scrupulous in paying tit for tat. Of all who led in stuffing the goose for the roasting, our American wit, Mr. E. H. House, excelled. He loved nothing better than to take these guileless and impressionable souls under his fatherly wing, lead them around, show them the sites and sights, both real and alleged, meanwhile filling the wallet of their imaginations — duly transferred, often on the spot, to notebooks — with the most astounding revelations. Many of their literary productions had no more basis than many of Lafcadio Hearn's generalizations that lead people to think of, and even to seek, in the land itself, a Japan that never, outside of dreams, existed. Nobody, more than House himself, enjoyed chuckling over his literary creations when they came out in books, or figured as strictly original contributions to comparative law, politics, religion, sociology and tomfoolery.

Mrs. Hepburn's experience as hostess was not at all unique, as many of us can testify. Some of her friends, on a birthday anniversary, had presented her with an unusually fine turkey. As she was to have an American newspaper correspondent at a dinner the next day, she had it cooked in honor of her guest and fellow countryman. This worthy knight of the fountain pen wrote home, to his syndicate, to tell how extravagant missionaries were; and, to spice his fiction, said that "the most luxurious meal he had had in his whole tour round the world was at a missionary's house and table." Alas, for the hotels at which the globe-encompassers must stay!

Baron Takahashi, now in 1913, Minister of Finance in the Cabinet of Premier Yamamoto, is one of the chief financiers of Japan. While negotiating the Russo-Japanese war loan, he wrote to me on June 3, 1905, as follows:

"I began to learn the alphabet under Mrs. Hepburn in 1864–65. Mr. Momotaro Sato and a few young students of the clan of Kaga were with me in her class of English."

Then he went on to tell of the Doctor's work as oculist, surgeon and general practitioner, and how it came to pass that he (Takahashi) did not become a physician.

"Dr. Hepburn had some medical students too. I remember Mr. Sato and I were once asked by one of them to catch a cat [one of the native bob-tailed variety] for the purpose of dissection. So one day we killed and brought in the animal to the Doctor, and the next morning we were called into the operating room to look on. But when I saw the procedure of dissection of the cat's eye, I was so horrified that I turned away for once and all from the medical profession."

Ambassador Hayashi wrote from London, to the writer, on January 29, 1903, five pages of his own recollections of Dr. and Mrs. Hepburn. He said:

"Whenever the 'customhouse officers,' as the local Japanese authorities [in Yokohama] were then called, met together and their conversation turned on topics connected with foreign residents and their affairs, Dr. Hepburn was invariably alluded to as 'Kun-shi,' a term signifying a superior man. This appellation, given as it was to a foreigner, at a time when all foreigners were universally regarded as aggressors, and accordingly were more or less hated by every class of people in Japan, goes far to prove how thoroughly the personality of Dr. Hepburn commanded the respect and consideration of all Japanese who came in contact with him.

"I was placed under the care of Mrs. Hepburn from 1862, at thirteen, until 1866, when I was sent to England for a course of study by the government of the Tokugawa.

"Doctor Hepburn was good, kind and humanely just, and he was unceasingly diligent, frugal and patient. Many of his patients were well-to-do, for his fame had gone abroad and men came from Yedo to consult him. At that time the journey required nearly a whole day, as the obstacles presented by ferries and guard gates on the road were so great.

His daily dispensary work took from three to five hours, according as his twenty or seventy patients needed. His whole afternoon was devoted to literary work in his study, excepting an hour or so before dinner, for his walk or his professional or private visits. The evening was spent in reading or conversation in the drawing room, and at ten o'clock the family retired.

"The lower class of Japanese who flocked to Yokohama to find employment as domestic servants with foreigners, were mostly unscrupulous men, almost the refuse of society, but the uniform kindness of Dr. and Mrs. Hepburn made them in many cases quite different men. One instance impressed itself upon my young mind. Dr. Hepburn had received from abroad for his dispensary some large bottles of alcohol. The servants in opening the box found one of these that was uncorked, and the Doctor heard them remarking to each other that the liquid smelled very much like 'shochu' [not saké, or rice beer, but strong liquor — distilled spirits] of the best quality. Their beaming eyes betrayed what was in their mind, and fearing lest they might be tempted to help themselves to it stealthily, he told them that these spirits were very much stronger than 'shochu,' and that they were only to be used for medical preparations. On no account were they to be drunk as 'shochu,' for they were powerful enough to kill a man, if so taken.

"That very night, the servants, four in all, conspired

to steal into the dispensary and they treated themselves to alcohol, diluted with water, to an extent seemingly far beyond their capacity; for they all reached such a state of inebriety that, losing the power of motion, they lay down on the spot quite unconscious and in a highly feverish condition. One of the servants was married, and his wife, noticing the long absence of her husband into the late hours of the night, felt anxious. In looking for him, she traced him to the dispensary. There finding him dying, as she supposed, she gave the alarm which brought the Doctor immediately to the rescue. Ordering the servants to be carried to their quarters, he gave directions to the woman to nurse them, attending them himself at frequent intervals.

"When they had quite recovered, the Doctor remonstrated with them, kindly but firmly, showing them that their actions constituted a theft, which in itself was very wicked. Apart from that, he had not warned them against drinking the liquid out of any niggardliness of disposition, but purely from the fear that they might be tempted to make themselves ill. The suffering and shame, therefore, which they had brought upon themselves was a just punishment. Thus he made their own consciences convict them. When the servants told me of this incident next day, they had tears in their eyes, and their love and regard for their master became redoubled. Henceforth, whatever they did, the welfare and interest of their master was almost always foremost in their minds.

I was very much impressed in observing what a force is exerted by kindness and sincerity over the hearts of these men, uneducated and unscrupulous though they were."

After four or five years with the Hepburns, Hayashi went to be a soldier for the Yedo shogun, his master. In the civil war, he was made prisoner and kept in the prison at Demma Cho, in Tokyo. As soon as Mrs. Hepburn heard of this, she came up from Yokohama and called on Hayashi's mother, expressing her sincere sympathy and thus truly comforted the old lady. "Though it was for but a short period, for a few years," said Mrs. Hepburn, "that I lived in the same house with your beloved son, yet I cannot even sleep at ease, every time I think of his miserable condition in prison."

For years after Hayashi left their home, the Hepburns spoke of him as their son.

"After more than twenty-five years of separation from Dr. and Mrs. Hepburn, I visited them again in 1893 in their new abode, on the Bluff in Yokohama," Count Hayashi continued his reminiscences. "I was pleased to find one of these servants still in the Doctor's service, he having been the youngest at the time of the incident referred to (on the preceding page). He was serving in as loyal and faithful a manner as ever. As I was told by Mrs. Hepburn, and as I found, he wrought with unabated regard and admiration for his master. I think he remained with the family until they left Japan for good."

MRS. HEPBURN

Whether the occasion was great or small Dr. and Mrs. Hepburn were always kind and considerate to all. Their life endeared them both to the Japanese of all classes. Count Hayashi said of Dr. Hepburn: "His duty as a missionary was not of a nature to admit of any thrilling incidents in his career, but his was one continual and unswerving application to his own conduct of the teachings which he spent the best part of his life in propagating in my country. His devotion to his duties made his life not less honored and noble, though perhaps less brilliant, than those of the world's most public men, whose actions may have commanded the admiration of mankind."

As for the golden memories recalled and words of affectionate appreciation spoken in the churches by native pastors, whose early training was at the feet of this Yokohama Gamaliel or his helpmate, we can cull only a few.

In the address of Rev. Yamano, at the opening of Shiloh church, in 1892, occurred these words:

"The feeling between parents and children is our feeling toward Dr. and Mrs. Hepburn. Verily they are our father and mother for the interest they take in us."

In his address, Mr. G. S. Ishikawa paid a remarkable compliment to Mrs. Hepburn: "Do you think Dr. Hepburn could have accomplished his grand work without his most faithful and courageous helpmeet? I positively declare 'No.' He could never have done it alone. At least half of his work should be credited to his most devoted wife."

To all of this, the man who knew best the facts could and did answer "Amen." The burden of his replies to the men's appreciations, which he received when about to leave Japan, in 1892, and which included his companion in life, was uniform. He made feeling answer, with variety in words but in substance one, as follows:

"No companion of any man could have done more than my wife." He said he had "always asked God to give him a good wife and his petition was more than answered."

Whether one approve or condemn Dr. Hepburn's opinions on coeducation, woman's suffrage and other agitating questions of the twentieth century, no one can deny that his happy personal experience formed the foundation for his rather conservative opinion and judgments.

XIII

THE GOLDEN KEY

IT is the glory of Christian missions that to-day in Japan the missionary physician is, in most places, hardly needed; for the Japanese themselves have so developed the arts and sciences of health and healing, that they can take care of their own people. The record of their medical and hygienic achievements at home and of the salvation of their wounded in war is surpassingly brilliant, and the world knows it well. In 1909 there were 1035 public hospitals in the empire; these — while costing only half as much as the hospitals of America — probably did as much good work. Of doctors there were 38,561, or eight to every 10,000 of the population; of midwives, 27,301; of pharmacists and druggists, 34,675.

Happy they who, following noble callings, yes, even the ministry of the gospel, labor for the good time coming when they themselves shall be no longer required. Divinely noble was the spirit of the prophet, who foretold the day when there would be no need of prophets, or teachers of the religion of Jehovah, for all should know God and their duty "from the least even to the greatest."

So far from being jealous of his pupils, Dr. Hepburn not only delighted in their success, but rejoiced to see from afar the day when he could close his dispensary and retire from dispensary work. He was all the more ready to do this because of the coming to Japan of Dr. J. C. Berry, missionary of the American Board for twenty-one years. Dr. Hepburn looked on Dr. Berry as one who, in a sense, should be his successor, carrying forth in the Kobe district the work he was about to lay down at Yokohama in order to give himself entirely to the task of translation.

Dr. Berry profited greatly by conversation with Dr. Hepburn as to methods of missionary work. He says: "The succeeding years of my life were very much influenced by this quiet, faithful, consecrated man. His work greatly enhanced the popular estimate of the work of medical missions and made the work even more easy and delightful." Dr. Berry tells then of his indebtedness to Dr. Hepburn by starting him on work as a specialist that in recent years has made him famous in America.

"Though skillful as a surgeon and physician, Dr. Hepburn was especially renowned in Japan as an oculist; and when I commenced work, it was assumed by the people that as Dr. Hepburn was an oculist, and an American physician, I being an American, must also know about the diseases of the eye. The result was large clinics of eye diseases at my hospitals and dispensaries, from the very first. . . . This necessitated special study on my part which, fol-

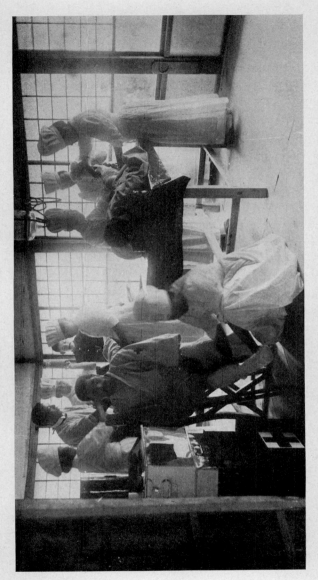

IN A MODERN JAPANESE OPERATING ROOM

lowed by an increase of my practice there, made it easy to qualify as a specialist in ophthalmology when I came away from Japan, and took up special study in Vienna."

When Dr. Hepburn deemed that medical knowledge in Japan had advanced sufficiently, he began his second and greater task, which will outlive, in its results, even the blessed work of healing the bodies of men. For — in the words of a Japanese orator — "by his dictionary, he made neighbors of distant nations." His book of words formed "the golden key" that opened the East to the West and the West to the East.

In the week after landing, in 1859, Dr. Hepburn began thirty-three years of systematic daily toil, glimpses of which I had the frequent honor and pleasure of seeing, when enjoying the boundless hospitality of his home, and discussing with him Japanese affairs. He seemed always glad to see me, for the point of view of a man in the capital, the center of purely native affairs, was usually quite different from that of one whose life was of necessity spent at the seaport, among the merchants and natives of the lower classes. At Yokohama any official present would resemble an oyster, rather than a bugle, in dispensing political information.

Realizing the necessity then of knowing the Japanese language not only in its perspective and growth and the polite speech of the cultured, but also the common people's vernacular, Dr. Hepburn listened to the plain folks and gathered up their idioms. He aspired to be able to read the entire Japanese literature, from the prehistoric time to the twentieth century. What this means, we in America can best understand by the statement, not lightly made, at the decease in 1912 of the late Rev. Walter W. Skeat, author of "An Etymological Dictionary of the English Language" and professor of Anglo-Saxon in the University of Cambridge. It was affirmed, by men knowing what they were saying, that he was "the only man who could read and understand the entire English language."

Dr. Hepburn read scores of Japanese novels, both historical and romantic, classic and ephemeral, select and vulgar. Such works as the "Glory and Fall of the Minamoto Family," the Héiké Monogotari, or Romance of the Héiké Clan, which come under the head of "classical fiction," and which all Japanese gentlemen and many of the educated women are expected to read, were his favorites. Knowing that— unless all history and human nature should be reversed —the majority of his hearers would be women and children, he devoured, for his Master's sake, hundreds of the cheap, popular storybooks. These were written in the *hira-kana*, or simple running script, which young people and the slightly educated could read. Though often repelled, as every clean-minded man must be, with the moral foulness and vile obscenity of many of these stories, he handled them very much as the farmer spreads manure —

not from any liking for the job, but for the sake of
the expected crop. He hoped, by the re-creating
and transmuting power of the Holy Spirit, to bring
forth out of the black mire of the pagan mind the
pure white lotus flower of Christianity. I confess
that while reading Japanese novels of the early day
I have more than once flung down in disgust the
filthy stuff whose obscenity lay on the surface, as
a top dressing, and was stored deeply all along the
literary route like the open cesspools so often seen
at the sides of the fields in rural Japan.

I remember being in the Doctor's study, when he
had just been reading that amazing and wonderful
record of the travels of Kidahachi and Yazirobéi
along the Tokaido, or Eastern Sea Road, from Yedo
to Kyoto. These two tramps, for such they were,
named their book Hizakurigé, that is, literally, Leg-
Hair, an idiom which corresponds to our "Shank's
Mare." Professor Chamberlain has characterized
this book as "the cleverest production of the Japanese
pen," and I am inclined to agree with this verdict.
It is an exceedingly naughty story, full of all kinds
of improper adventures, and sometimes the literary
condiment approaches a piquancy not calculated to
minister either to sound spiritual digestion, or to
the edifying of the nobler part of man. Yet its wit,
humor, shrewd judgments, bright-colored descrip-
tions and most amusing episodes — all given with
the rapid movement of a picture-play — make it
one of the most readable of Japanese books. As a

mirror of life, on the most traveled road in the empire, in the old days of the daimios, it has not been surpassed. Its text is hardly translatable, nor is it probable that the translation — even if possible — would ever be a paying proposition, even if expurgated and fumigated, for the glorious days of the ever-crowded and busy highway of the Tokaido are forever over. The abolition of feudalism, the new commercial life, the habits of travel by steamer and railway have relegated the Eastern Sea Road, once as lively as a county fair, to shady desuetude.

We laughed over some of the odd adventures of the redoubtable walkers, and agreed that, apart from the literary fascination of the book and its power to touch both fancy and imagination, it was a rich storehouse of local idiom and dialectical peculiarities. Several trips over the Tokaido afterwards, made its word-pictures even more vivid.

Thus the Doctor, mastering all levels of the native speech, was able, in the dispensary, his Bible class, his ministrations in prayer meeting and in pulpit, to talk "in a tongue understanded of the people," and to bring home Christian truths in a manner to be quickly apprehended and deeply cherished. He welcomed knowledge from every source, and his familiarity with science, history and literature made him an ideal lexicographer and translator.

It seems a curious fact that he who could for so many years speak with sufficient and engaging fluency in Japanese, should at times, when at home, so dis-

trust himself in the public use of his native tongue.
Even in boyhood days, the question came up as to
his ability to speak in public, when deciding upon
the choice of a career. Pleading at the bar, or usefulness in the pulpit would require some oratorical
power, which he — as boy or man — never possessed.
Even in the maturity of his powers, he more than once
lost faith in himself to speak acceptably to an audience. In later years American Christians were
hungry for news from Japan, specially when the
prospects of the kingdom's coming were very dark.
On one occasion, while visiting his home, he was
induced, almost by main force, to enter a pulpit to
speak. When the time came for him to speak, he
rose, trembling, and succeeded three times in getting as far as to say "My dear friends." Then
he retreated and sat down, refusing to get up
again!

Nevertheless, having five talents, instead of ten,
he buried none. As teacher and in council and
where speech, not of an oratorical, but of a delibera-
tive kind was required, he always delivered his
thoughts with force and clarity, speaking with
brevity and to the point. He reminded one of Dr.
John Hall in council, whose every word seemed to
weigh a pound. It is certain that he was a model
to brethren inclined to follow the track of the Meander
River.

This tireless student rose every day at five o'clock
in the morning and in cold weather made his own

fire. He worked until breakfast time, which was between seven and eight. Then followed family worship, after which he took a short stroll, then he went into the dispensary, usually for an hour, but sometimes for three or four hours. In addition to the usually crowded front room, there was another back of it, which, besides chairs for the patients who were called in one by one for treatment, was well provided with shelves for medicine, and for Chinese Bibles and tracts. These latter, in time, gave way to the same blessed messages in easily read Japanese. Returning to his study, he worked on his dictionary, or his reading in Japanese literature, and, in later days, on his translation or revision of the Bible, until dinner time, at one o'clock. In the afternoons he would take his exercise and attend to the innumerable calls, medical, evangelical, social, or to multifarious public services. The evening was usually spent in light work, or in fulfilling social demands.

So it came to pass that, to the surprise and delight of a small but eagerly waiting public, he got out the first edition of his great dictionary, on which all others are based, as early as 1867. The art of printing by means of metal type not having yet been introduced among the Japanese, he went to Shanghai, and there spent several months reading proof and overseeing the printing. The work was done at the Presbyterian Mission Press, which has been as a great lighthouse in modern China. Its output for the enlightenment of the Far East cannot be measured till eternity dawns. Its widening influence can be compared only to the ever-increasing wavelets which circle from the central pebble.

In his preface he says that only two printed works, in Japanese — the Japanese-Portuguese dictionary published in 1603, compiled by a Jesuit missionary, and a small Japanese vocabulary by Dr. Medhurst, printed in Batavia, in 1830 — then existed. There was indeed, in the early sixties, one English and Japanese dictionary, compiled by the Satsuma scholars, but this was only for natives of Japan. Dr. Hepburn fixed the definitions in English, making Japanese the basis.

When an invoice of the completed dictionary arrived in Yokohama, there was excitement indeed. Old residents could scarcely believe their own eyes. The new situation was as thrilling as the revelation in a moment of a vast landscape, a Darien-peak view. It enabled men thus to see, as it were, two continents joined — rather, perhaps, solid land and boundless ocean made one. Two worlds, as by an isthmus, seemed to have been united. Perhaps we might liken it to the Panama Canal ready for operation. As for a rapid feat of intellect and industry, it seemed a *tour de force*, a Marathon run. The well-trained spiritual athlete, despite a frail body, had tossed and floored all obstacles one after another.

The translator was able to pay his printing, boarding and travel expenses from the sale of the first edition of his great work, but scarcely more. In the hands of the dealers and those who had copies, the price steadily rose. When the Elder Statesmen and politicians of to-day — the power behind the throne — were as yet young students, I well remember how valued and prized this book was among them, for I knew them all. When I arrived in Yokohama in 1870, and sought to purchase Hepburn's dictionary, the price demanded at one store was thirty-two dollars, but from a friend, who had a spare copy, I secured one for eighteen dollars. I afterwards heard that sixty-two dollars was paid for a copy in ordinary binding.

Since that time, other dictionaries in French, German, Italian, Dutch and Russian, and — for aught I know to the contrary — in other languages, have appeared. Indeed, some say there are at least twenty in foreign tongues now on the market, in addition to the score or more of dictionaries made by the Japanese. But no maker of any dictionary, explaining or translating the Japanese, could afford to ignore the work which Dr. Hepburn did. One of the secretaries of the Japanese Legation at Washington wrote to me recently, as follows: "Indeed I may say what every Japanese will agree with me in saying, that the dictionaries which followed his were in fact merely revised editions of his work."

Dr. Hepburn's first business dealings with a Japanese publisher were not such as to confirm the hopes of those who trusted either in the rapid rise in reputation of Japan's commercial integrity, or the actual improvement in morals of the native dealers. In one case, in 1883, a native bookseller, — who had evidently made a handsome thing from the sale of the dictionaries — felt himself greatly injured by the Doctor's publishing in New York an abridged edition of his great work. He declared that he would be revenged on the lexicographer — as the Doctor wrote — "by republishing, with improvements, any new edition of my dictionary I may bring out. This matter of selling my dictionary to him and putting myself in his power has been a very great mistake and sorrow to me." His later relations with the highly enterprising and honorable firm of Z. P. Maruya & Co., of Tokyo, were wholly satisfactory.

A second edition of the dictionary appeared in 1872, printed in Shanghai as before. It was when in New York, in 1873, that the Doctor brought out an abridged edition of this work. About the same time, amid the heat of a Manhattan summer, he transliterated in Roman characters the translation into Japanese of the Gospel of John. The American Bible Society published it, interleaved with the English version.

On May 7, 1886, he finished the revision of his third edition and obtained government copyright, through Z. P. Maruya & Co. The profits from this edition were large, since so many thousands of Japanese were eagerly studying English, and missionaries in Japan were now as numerous as a regiment of soldiers. So the Doctor was able to assist liberally the Shiloh church and the Méiji Gaku-in, or college, in Tokyo. Having entered fully into the spirit of Jesus, he found by joyful experience, that it was "more blessed to give than to receive." This liberality in giving characterized him all through life. After his death, when I went into his study at East Orange, New Jersey, I found it incredibly bare. He had given everything away that could be useful to anyone else. Taking the promises of God seriously, he had lent all to the Lord.

Before going over to China to print the first edition of his dictionary, he made himself ready for new opportunities to open men's hearts. There was an even easier and quicker way of reaching individuals and sowing the seed of the Word: this was by means of the tract. Scattered as from the sower's hand, millions of these leaves would fall upon the hard wayside, on the thin soil of rocky ground, amid thorns — furnishing food only for the birds of jest and indifference — or amid the hideous thorns of real enmity. Nevertheless, where the lifeholding germs found hidden lodgment in honest hearts, there would be a return, thirty, sixty and a hundred fold; of this the Doctor might hear only in later years, and often not at all.

Dr. Hepburn began his work in the literature of tracts by translating one written in Chinese, by Divie Bethune McCartee, M.D., called "A True Doctrine Explained." He had wooden blocks secretly cut in Yokohama, and then sent them to Shanghai in 1867 to be printed. This was the first Christian tract published in the Japanese Empire. Five thousand copies were issued. In 1874, he translated and published a little tract called "The Sweet Sad Story of the Cross."

Later on, he put into Japanese and published the Westminster Shorter Catechism, and the Confession of Faith. With the coöperation of Rev. Edward Rothesay Miller, he translated the Form of Government of the Union Church of Japan. Later on, as a member of the Bible Revising Committee, he revised Rev. J. Piper's translation of the books of Jonah, Haggai and Malachi, and prepared them for publication by the Bible Society, and also the Book of Joshua, done into Japanese by the Rev. Mr. Fyson. In 1880 he transliterated into the Roman letter the whole New Testament and published it in Yokohama, for the American Bible Society. In 1881 he was engaged in translating the book of Proverbs.

Thus in the medical art, in literature, and in Bible translation, James Curtis Hepburn built imperishable memorials in Japan. Yet the greatest monument — more like a lighthouse, with lamps ever trimmed and burning and pulsing out its beams of life-saving light afar — is the monument of character which he left. One who lived long among missionaries and met with many types of human beings in several countries wrote me concerning Dr. Hepburn:

"Zeal and work are great things, but in the long run it is character that tells; and in what high and homely, what lofty and intimate strains has been sung the life song of this man, — physician, translator, teacher, author and Christian gentleman!"

XIV

A RAILWAY THROUGH THE NATIONAL INTELLECT

THE first of first things for a Christian missionary is to give the people the Word of God in their own tongue. Yet this very first thing cannot be done immediately, for man is finite. He must patiently learn the vernacular of those among whom he lives. A day of Pentecost cannot be improvised for each and every individual. Like the landscape of mountains and plains — nature in variety — there is a higher and a lower form of speech, a spoken and a written language, and both must be mastered. The real perils and possible pitfalls of unpleasant mental associations must be avoided, the mire of infelicity leaped or quickly passed, and the eternal proprieties made the law of translation. Surely no Panama Canal, no railway up Mount Washington, or bridging of the St. Lawrence or Zambesi rivers requires bolder engineering or finer skill.

The story of the Bible in Japanese, as given by Dr. Hepburn, at the public celebration of the completion of the New Testament in the great meeting held in Tokyo, April 19, 1880, is probably the best extant. It is a romantic story of perseverance and discouragement, of indomitable industry and of victory over many obstacles. Though no numerous or extensive attempts at translation of the Holy Scriptures were made before the modern opening of Japan, the history of these is very interesting.

The Doctor wrote of these: "It is not known that the Roman Catholic missionaries in Japan between 1549 and 1587, — that is, between the arrival of Francis Xavier and the edict of expulsion, — translated and published any portions of the Bible, and this notwithstanding they had full liberty of speech and met with no political hindrances to their work. They translated the Ten Commandments and the Lord's Prayer, and probably some of the narrative portions of the Old Testament, and some of the Psalms and parables, and portions of the New Testament sufficient for their liturgical worship; but nothing remains now that we know of. Their work did not survive probably the scrutiny and destruction of the Japanese Government. In the religious books published for the use of the native converts free use was made of Latin terms, such as *Deus, gratia, animus, sanctus, spiritu, inferno, iglesia, filio, baptismo,* etc."

In modern times the first known translation of any part of the Bible into Japanese was, as we have seen, by the Prussian, Rev. Karl Gutzlaff, in connection with the Netherlands Mission Society, in 1827. He came to Siam in 1832, and was afterwards Colonial Secretary at Hong Kong, where he translated the New Testament into Chinese. His knowledge of the Japanese language was gained largely through ship-wrecked sailors, of whom there has always been a constant supply on the Asiatic coast.

In 1880, Dr. Hepburn holding up this rare biblio-graphical treasure, Gutzlaff's version, said: "This is undoubtedly the first effort to render the Word of life into Japanese, and though exceedingly imperfect and abounding with errors, it cannot but be regarded by every Christian heart with respect."

Some specimens of the ideas and dialect of the sailors, as used by Gutzlaff, were given. The word for God was *Gokuraku*, which the Buddhists use for Paradise, or the state of supreme bliss. For *logos*, or the Word, he used an expression meaning a wise or clever person. For Holy Spirit, the term employed is *kami*, which means simply superior, and is a very inadequate expression for anything divine.

About the same time Dr. S. Wells Williams met with one or two Japanese sailors and with their aid translated the book of Genesis and perhaps one of the Gospels. In 1860 he sent these in manuscript to Dr. Hepburn, but they were never published, and were burned in the fire which destroyed Dr. S. R. Brown's house in 1867. Happily these Japanese friends of Dr. Williams were so influenced in their work on the Scriptures that they became Christians and adorned the doctrine they believed.

The next translator was a Hungarian Hebrew, Rev. B. J. Bettelheim, M.D., who was sent by the Naval Mission to the Riu Kiu Islands. Despite his great strength of mind and body, he succumbed at last to the insults, annoyances and intimidation to which he was subjected by the authorities and left in 1854, living for a time in Chicago. He is believed to have made a translation of the whole New Testament in the Riu Kiu (Loo Choo) dialect, and while in Hong Kong published the Gospel of Luke on blocks, in royal octavo size, with Gutzlaff's translation in Chinese at the top of the page and his own, in the Riu Kiu dialect, at the bottom in *kata-kana*. Afterwards, Dr. Bettelheim revised his work in Chicago with the assistance of a Japanese, and so brought it into conformity with the pure Japanese. This revision, consisting of the four Gospels and Acts in the script, called *hira-kana*, or running hand, was printed at Vienna, in 1872, for the British and Foreign Bible Society, and a good many copies were sent to Japan, but probably these were little read. Thus the pioneers — amid enormous labors, on a thorny path and in noble spirit — made a beginning.

All the first missionaries after the Harris treaty of 1859 saw the necessity of putting the gospel into Japanese. Dr. Hepburn began the work as early as 1861, but such was the prejudice against Christianity at that time and so great the fear of the government, that his teacher, after proceeding a little way in the Gospel of Matthew, positively declined to help him further and left his service. In later years this man entered the Christian Church. Dr. S. R. Brown, beginning in 1856, lost all his manuscripts in the fire of 1867. Dr. Hepburn and Rev. Messrs. Ballagh and Thompson met in the dispensary and spent nine months on the Gospel of Matthew, and Dr. David Thompson attempted the book of Genesis in 1869, but none of these translations were printed.

The Baptist missionaries led the way in actual publication. Rev. Jonathan Goble, formerly a marine in Commodore Perry's service, issued his rude translation of Matthew, in the autumn of 1871, in *hira-kana*, which was the first of any of the books of the Bible that were published in the empire. He said: "I tried in Yokohama to get the blocks cut for printing, but all seemed afraid to undertake it, and I was only able to get it done in Tokyo, by a man who, I think, did not know the nature of the book he was working upon."

One of the wonderful feats of translation in modern times was the rendering of the whole of the New Testament in Japanese, by the veteran missionary, Rev. Nathan Brown. In 1880 Dr. Hepburn congratulated "our Baptist brethren assembled here to-day. They have an especial cause, also, for rejoicing in the completion of their version by that veteran missionary and our friend, Dr. Nathan Brown, who having accomplished a similar work for the natives of Assam, has the honor also of having completed the translation of the New Testament into this language and publishing it some months previous to this committee."

Before 1870, Dr. Hepburn had translated the four Gospels with the help of Okuno, and these were revised by Dr. S. R. Brown and himself, with Okuno's assistance, and published: Mark and John in the autumn of 1872, and Matthew in the spring of 1873.

In September, 1872, the Protestant missionary societies, then represented in Japan, made provision to translate the Bible. The committee, consisting of Messrs. Brown, Hepburn and Greene, did not meet until June, 1874. The other missions, including the English and American Episcopal and Père Nicolai of the Greek Church, were invited to coöperate. Rev. Nathan Brown sat with the committee about eighteen months, until January, 1876. On November 3, 1879 — five years and six months after they had begun their work of translating and revising — the New Testament appeared in public.

The translators determined to seek a golden mean between the quasi-Chinese style, only intelligible to the highly educated, and the vulgar colloquial; they wanted a medium respected even by the so-called literati, but also easy and intelligible to all classes. Therefore, they adhered to the vernacular, or pure Japanese, and to a style which may be called classic, in which many of their best books intended for the common reader are written.

Of the Japanese helpers, Okuno, Takahashi, Miwa

and Matsuyama, the latter was with the committee from the first and throughout the whole work. He was the chief dependant, assistant and arbiter in all cases of difficulty. "Whatever virtue there is in our Japanese text," said Dr. Hepburn, in 1880, "it is mainly, if not altogether, owing to his scholarly ability, the perfect knowledge he has of his own language, his conscientious care and his identifying himself with the work; and as a committee, we feel under especial obligations to him and extend to him our hearty thanks."

Dr. Hepburn declared that there was no foreigner in the country who had such a knowledge of the Japanese language as would enable him, working alone, to bring out an idiomatic and good translation without the aid of a native scholar, and the literary merit of a translation would depend principally upon the ability and scholarship of his native assistants.

The traditional hostility of the government to Christianity and the impossibility of getting native printers to undertake the work sufficiently explain why the Scriptures, even in portions, were not published until 1872, in which year the anti-Christian edicts were removed.

The members of the original committee of 1872 were engaged for a year on the first eleven chapters of Genesis. It consisted of the two Browns (S. R. and Nathan), Greene, Quimby, Maclay, Cochran, Piper, Wright, Waddell, Goble, Krecker and Hepburn. To facilitate the work, portions of the Old Testament were assigned to local committees of missionaries residing in eight different ports and cities. After long experience, it was found that this plan did not succeed well, and at a meeting in January, 1882, the permanent committee appointed three of its members, Verbeck, Tyson and Hepburn, to do the main work. These were joined later by three Japanese brethren, Matsuyama, Uyémura and Ibuka, but their want of acquaintance with the original text was fatal to the best results, and the Japanese committee finally dissolved, of its own accord, in 1886.

One by one, or in twos and threes, the books of the Old Testament came out for publication. Despite sickness, absence, pressure of other labors, and interruptions innumerable and unnameable, the work went on. Happily, these very difficulties and obstacles were transformed, as by miracle, into aids and encouragements, for greater uniformity of style was secured and the translations of the various books were made into an unexpected and striking unity.

In mid-February, 1871, I had the opportunity and the high honor of being the first to carry into the far interior of Japan the four Gospels in Japanese. I was to go into the province of Echizen, on the west coast, and in the city of Fukui, to organize schools on the American system of public education. Echizen lay in front of the capital, Kyoto, but behind the mountains, and the city was the

[144]

stronghold of Buddhism. When I was ready to start, the Doctor had so far progressed in his mastery of the language and translation of the Bible that he was enabled to hand me, with his blessing, a manuscript copy of the four Gospels in Japanese. Thus it came to pass that I carried the first translation of the Gospels beyond the jealously guarded line of the treaty ports into the interior and at once began teaching a Bible class in my own house on Sunday mornings.

It has been the hope of some of the most bigoted of the official class to keep all knowledge of Christianity from leaking into the country at large. An occasional hint was given me that I had better not attempt to teach Christianity in Fukui. In that day, at every ferry and market place, along the highroads, at the village entrances, and in the cities stood the stone platforms containing, inscribed on boards, the government edicts. These denounced the "corrupt religion of Jesus Christ," with the offer of government gold to all who would inform on followers of the accursed sect, or its teachers. Into the privacy or sanctity of my own home, however, I never allowed any Japanese, high or low, to insert even the thin end of the wedge of suggestion of right or power. On the other hand, I am bound to say that I never raised even the American flag over my house, or made any outward action that would in any way seem to trespass upon the generous hospitality shown me, without inquiring of the authorities whether such were agreeable, and that I paid scrupulous attention to all external public requirements.

In "The Mission News" of May 27, 1905, Dr. D. C. Greene wrote of his coworking with Dr. Hepburn in translating the Bible. He said:

"In some respects it was a difficult position for us both. He was my senior by well-nigh thirty years. Our training had been different and naturally our points of view did not always coincide. Sometimes the methods of his young colleague must have seemed iconoclastic to Dr. Hepburn, and no doubt they were often ill chosen. Both of us held pronounced opinions, which, upon occasion, were forcibly expressed; but, in spite of all, we worked well together and very rarely were we obliged to refer a question in dispute to our colleagues. Indeed, I cannot recall a single question which we did not succeed in settling by ourselves, though not always to our complete satisfaction."

It was a thrilling epoch in the life of Dr. Hepburn, when, after ten years of labor, the New Testament in Japanese was ready for the nation and empire. Such an event might be in its celebration as modest as the advent of a Bethlehem babe in the manger, though in the sweep of its significance, it might throw battles and campaigns into shadow and oblivion. No legate of the Mikado or the government was in the Japanese church in Tokyo, when, on April 19, 1880, the representatives of fourteen missionary societies using the English language and

DR. HEPBURN IN 1880
At the time of the completion of his translation
of the New Testament into Japanese

of all the Protestant churches in the capital were assembled to celebrate the completion of the New Testament translation into Japanese.

Most of the exercises were in Japanese, including the singing of hymns, "Nearer My God to Thee," "Rock of Ages" and "Hold the Fort." Rev. Nathan Brown, who had made revisions of the whole New Testament into two languages, read the Nineteenth Psalm. Prayer was offered by the translator, Rev. John Piper of the English Church Missionary Society.

Dr. Verbeck's address was in the language of the country. He told of the various attempts to give the Mikado's people the New Testament in their own tongue. He then outlined the great work and organization of the Bible Societies, in Great Britain and the United States, all of which showed the true unity of all believers in the God of the Bible. He fitly closed his address, as he so often on other occasions felicitously did, with a quotation from the Japanese, "Though diverse the ways of ascent, it is the same moon that is beheld from the lofty mountain tops."

Okuno Masatusuna made no reference to his own part in the work of translation, but showed the superiority of the Word of God to all the philosophies of Greece, the prowess of Rome, and the boasted achievements of science in modern days. His text was "This is the Lord's doing, and it is marvellous in our eyes." His powers of reasoning and of illustration were the more remarkable because, though well instructed in the principles of Christianity, he was not acquainted with any European language. An eloquent man like Apollos, and mighty in the Scriptures, himself a living exhibition of the power of the truth which seems to clothe its possessor, he swayed his auditors as the mountain breezes bend the ripe rice stalks in autumn.

This address was followed by a prayer in Japanese by Mr. Ogawa, a native pastor, one of the very first laborers in the translation of the Gospels into Japanese, a noble monument of the grace of God in Christ Jesus, beloved of all.

Dr. Hepburn in speaking showed that "it is especially to bring the Bible and make known its teachings, that the Christian missionary comes to this land or goes to any land." After showing the failure of Buddhism and Confucianism, he laid open the actual facts of paganism.

"In vain we look in these countries (China, Japan and Korea) for a healthy public sentiment against lying and deceit, licentiousness and intemperance, for civil liberty and relief from the oppression and cruelty of arbitrary power, for manliness, independence and assertion of political rights. Nor do we see, as the outcome of Confucianism and Buddhism, hospitals provided for the sick, or asylums for the poor, infirm and the outcast."

Then he went on to notice the sudden awakening from the sleep of centuries and the rapid introduction amongst the Japanese of the fruits of their civilization, which Western nations have wrought out. Again he spoke fearlessly truths not always palatable in Japan and apparently unknown to the flatterers of paganism and those who to-day minister to native vanity by caricaturing history.

In this nation, neither Confucianism nor Buddhism has had anything to do with these improvements. They rather spring from a peculiar national ambition, versatility of character, and readiness to imitate and adopt whatever appears to constitute superiority in others. "But without the Bible and the foundation which it lays deep in the hearts of the people, we may well tremble for the beautiful superstructure which they are raising, lest it come tumbling down as quickly as it has gone up. The Bible is what this nation now needs above all other things."

Urging diligence, without haste and without rest, in the further work of putting the whole Bible into Japanese, he closed by saying:

"May the day soon come, when we shall meet together to celebrate this most desirable event — the translation of the whole Bible into Japanese."

Happy man! He did live to see the end crown the work.

XV

UNCEASING INDUSTRY

IN the journal kept by Dr. Hepburn from 1880 to 1895, the entries are scanty, but significant. From his first arrival in Yokohama he kept a record of the temperature, and this ultimately became of great value. The biographer made use of these observations and published them in a condensed form, in an appendix to the first edition of "The Mikado's Empire," in 1876. When the Japanese Meteorological Bureau was established, which furnished the weather probabilities daily, often predicting storms and earthquakes, as well as other expected occurrences, he gave up this full record as being no longer needed. He, however, made notes on natural phenomena. For example, he told of the bursting into bloom of the magnolias, camellias, peach and cherry trees, and of his going out to see them.

The instances are not infrequent of Dr. Hepburn's sickness "in bed," "with a severe cold," etc., which showed how careful this tireless worker had to be to preserve health and strength.

He acted as elder for many years in the Union Church at Yokohama, being repeatedly reëlected, in spite of his desire to decline. For a time a brilliant Canadian, Rev. Geo. Cochran, acted as pastor. On February 25, 1887, "Rev. Mr. Underwood arrived from Korea to publish his translation of the Gospel by Mark."

The fact was noted that Rev. Mr. Correll's twin children were baptized and one of them was named after Mrs. Hepburn, Ethel Hepburn Correll — one of many in the missionary household in Japan who bore this good woman's name.

On April 15, 1887, the faculty of the Méiji Gaku-in (Hall of Learning of the Era of Enlightened Government), in Tokyo, notified Dr. Hepburn, by letter, that he had been elected president of the institution and appointed to the chair of Physiology and Hygiene. After a visit to Tokyo, to examine into the working of the Méiji Gaku-in, he wrote accepting the position of president of the institution and the chair of Physiology and Hygiene.

The tender sympathies of the diarist were thus revealed on April 19, 1887: "Tony von der Huyde, born July 9, 1872, died this morning. She was a member of my wife's Sunday school and much beloved for her gentle, affectionate and intelligent character. She was an only child and has flown away to the Beautiful Land, leaving her parents desolate and heartbroken. O Death, how sad thou art! But the Second Adam has conquered thee and broken thy bands! Glory be unto Christ our Lord!"

Here I may insert a snapshot picture made by a

lady — one among the first of Christian American children born in Japan. It is her impression of the "old Doctor."

"After many years' absence, I was again a frequent visitor in his house, this time on the Bluff. Mrs. Hepburn was conducting a Sunday-school class of the children of foreign residents, but the Doctor was never able to inspire the least awe in those dainty little people. They loved him, but they could not fear him.

"Only two months after, in a hotel in Guadalajara, Mexico, Lady A——, of London, said to me, 'You knew the Hepburns? Lovely people! They entertained me so kindly, when I visited Japan before the China-Japan war.' Just so! The command 'Be careful to entertain strangers' they obeyed literally. Nor was this the light matter it might appear. On the highroad of oriental travel, their house became a sort of Mecca. People with letters of introduction and people without, people interested in missions and people who scoffed at them, came to the Hepburns in passing, and all united in admiration for these kindly old residents. Intensely human, with infinite appreciation of young life, the Doctor said to a couple of young people, who were among the hundreds of guests at his jubilee reception, 'Have you found the lovers' bower upstairs?'"

To resume the diary story: On April 24, 1887, this entry was made:

"This day, twenty-eight years ago, sailed from New

York to come to Japan. Of the eleven friends that came to say farewell when we left, six are dead. The future was then to us a perfect blank. We only knew that the Lord was leading us. Now that I can look back on these twenty-eight years, what a history of God's love and power and his guidance and care of us and of his work toward this nation!"

On May 9, 1887, Dr. and Mrs. Hepburn went to Nikko, renting one of the priest's houses for three months, till the first of July.

On July 25, 1887, the Doctor went to Nikko for six days, enjoying the cool nights, where a blanket was needed, and where "mosquitoes were few and not very savage." The railway enabled him now to reach this gem of the Almighty's workmanship, well named "Sunny Splendor," — in hours as few as formerly days were many. He stayed from August 13 to September 8. He wrote: "Our litttle dog 'Doc' died on August 30, having been sick some three weeks."

On October 7, 1887, Anne Hepburn Ballagh was married to Rev. Robert Eugene McAlpine. (The biographer, in an address, before the Bible Training School in New York on March 20, 1913, on the centenary of David Livingstone, met their oldest daughter preparing for missionary service.) On October 28, 1887, Rev. Young J. Allen arrived from Shanghai, and on November 28, Dr. H. N. Allen (first medical missionary and afterwards United States plenipotentiary in Korea) called.

On December 14, 1887, after giving details of translation, revision, transliteration and preparing for the press, Dr. Hepburn made his record:

"Have thus finished my work on translating and printing the Holy Scriptures. Thanks be to my God and Saviour who has given me the health to help me in the work and permitted me to see it finished. Praise be to His holy name."

On December 31, 1887, Dr. Hepburn received from the Scotch Bible Society a copy of the whole Bible in Japanese — the first to be put into proper clothing and attractive binding. On December 25, we find him getting ready for his work in the Méiji Gaku-in, in which institution he began teaching January 10, making entry:

"I gave a lecture on Man, his position in this world and his relation to matter. I found my lecture was far above the comprehension of my class, who are sophomores. So I must come to using a simple book."

On January 20, 1888, Dr. Hepburn wrote:

"Had a meeting of the Permanent Committee and resigned our duties as a translation and revising committee. . . . Our work on the translation of the sacred Scriptures is finished. Fifteen years since the work was commenced in 1872, as authorized by that convention, though thirteen years since the work on the New Testament was actually commenced in the committee! I am the only member of that committee now in Japan. The two Doctor Browns resting from their work! Drs. Greene and Maclay at home!"

On the next day, February 3, "the completion of the translation of the Bible into Japanese was celebrated in the Shin Sakai church in Tokyo. Dr. Verbeck and Dr. Cochran and myself made addresses."

"Feb. 16, 1888. In bed with lumbago."

Ever in close contact with life on its physical side, the Doctor was interested in the relation of population to food supply, for he knew well about the frequent famines which in old hermit days had desolated Japan, sometimes carrying off over a million in a year. He noted in February, 1888, that the annual yield of rice in the empire was 30,000,000 *koku* (roughly 75,000,000 bushels), which at five yen per *koku* would yield 150,000,000 yen (dollars then, now half dollars). The area of the rice fields was 5,850,000 acres, the yield per acre being about $251\frac{1}{2}$ bushels. In other words, on an archipelago fitted by nature to support about eight or ten millions only, over fifty millions of people must, in the twentieth century, find food and gain a living. Only a certain proportion, say one tenth, of the soil of Japan can be cultivated. Japan must become even more industrial and maritime in order to buy food and to maintain her existence. This problem is one for statesmen, while at the same time the over-busy war-makers and money-lenders in the United States and elsewhere find reason, in these facts, for crying up their trade of blood-letting, in order to make money.

On March 13, 1888, the Doctor wrote:

"The seventy-third anniversary of my birth! I

find my physical condition gradually deteriorating. I am now so full of rheumatic pains in my back and legs, I have had to give up walking, which I can now do only with pain. This affects my spirits. I now teach physiology in the Méiji Gaku-in twice a week and am adding references to the Old Testament. This, with my Sunday Bible class, of forty or more, constitutes my work at present."

On October 17, 1888, he visited the steam yacht *Coronet*, on which were Professor and Mrs. Todd, the latter of whom has written so charmingly of the voyage and scientific results in her book, "Corona and Coronet."

In spite of his rheumatism, which later became, as he wrote on June 18, 1888, "gout in both feet," the Doctor's journal contains many records of journeys to and from the capital and cities, at which he attended meetings of the synods and conferences on affairs of the Church and the ever-coming kingdom. The problems were now those of expansion and success and of open doors; not of discouragement or patient waiting, as of old.

In the statistics for January 19, 1884, as given in the meeting, at Dr. Hepburn's house, of the Tract Society's Committee, there were then in Japan eighty-six Protestant churches, with six thousand members, and four religious papers.

February 11, 1889, was a day of popular rejoicing throughout all Japan. On that day, according to popular allegation and official pronouncement and in

THE MIKADO

Japanese ways of thinking, the Emperor "granted a constitution to his people." In the idea and idiom of the continent of America, and in simple fact, nearly two centuries of thought and over twenty-one years of intense political agitation had resulted in the thinking men of Japan's obtaining a form of government better fitted to the age and condition of the country. The happy event was overclouded by the brutal assassination of the Minister of Education, Arinori Mori, by one of those murderers who have been vastly too numerous in the country. Their breed is even yet perpetuated by popular admiration — whereas, the type ought long since to have been removed from the face of the earth.

On February 13, 1889, the Doctor noted the beginning of his Bible dictionary.

Perhaps the literary work which Dr. Hepburn most enjoyed personally and at which he wrought with minutely loving care, was this Bible dictionary in Japanese, which he brought out in 1891. Knowing that the heavenly treasure of divine revelation was embedded in earthen vessels that were odd, queer and strange, to the Japanese, he longed to furnish to them as many as possible of the side lights of information, and true reflections of their own manners and customs; that is, the "Orientalisms," which enabled them to understand the message and the meaning of incidents and action recorded in the sacred text. With this book in his hand, the native Christian elder, church officer, teacher, or the Bible reader, has had his way into the minds of those whom he desired to benefit, made smoother. To translate the Bible into Japanese was like building a road through the national intellect. While the blasting of the rocks, the leveling of the forest, the filling up of the swamps, and the making of levels and gradients were all important, yet the building of bridges, switches, stations and signals were scarcely less necessary for actual use and benefit. And in this, as in so many other things, Dr. Hepburn was a pioneer, and his work is of unique value. "Missionary Efficiency" — a vital topic nowadays — reached almost its acme in him.

Notices of the passing away of "old-time student volunteers," comrades and friends who had been with him in the mission field, or of whom he had known well, became painfully numerous as the years advanced. Noticeable was the decease of D. B. Simmons, M.D., on February 19, 1889. This fellow brother in science and the art of healing had come out as medical missionary of the Reformed Church in 1859. After severing his connection with the Board, he entered the medical service of the Japanese, organized hospitals and made a noble record in Japan's great army of the Yatoi (or salaried helpers).

"Feb. 16, 1884. Dr. S. Wells Williams died this evening in New Haven at 8:40. I first met him in Macao in 1843, June 9. We have lived together, corresponded, and often met since that day. Had a warm love for each other. He was a true friend, a joyous Christian and lover of Christ's kingdom. Born in Utica, September 22, 1812, he came to China October 25, 1833." Dr. Williams' book "The Middle Kingdom" is even yet, all things considered, the best all-round work on China.

"Oct. 1, 1884. Went to Tokyo to a dinner given by the Tokyo Medical Society. Some seventy doctors sat down to dinner. Heard several very animated speeches from Japanese and others. This is one of the evidences of the wonderful advance made by this nation. How little I thought, twenty-five years ago, that I should see such a sight in my day."

In 1892 after thirty-three years of loving service, Dr. Hepburn, the Christ-filled pilgrim, retired from active toil, to spend his remaining days in his native land. "But," a writer in the Japan "Evangelist" said, "he left upon many Japanese, some of whom are statesmen of high position to-day, im-pressions for good that will never die. He was larger than his great church, larger than any one denomination — he belonged to us all. It was not his books that made us love him, though these are indispensable; not his gift of healing, though we thank him for that; not the churches or halls, though these be useful; it is the large, symmetrical Christian man that we admired and loved."

XVI

THE COMPLETED BIBLE IN JAPANESE

TWO documents of supreme importance to Japan, closely related to each other, both completed and given to the world in the month of February, the one in 1888 and the other in 1889, were the Bible in Japanese and the National Constitution. Both were promulgated and celebrated in Tokyo, the capital. In a very real sense, and in very close relation to each other, both had much their same time of secret growth — "first the blade, then the ear, then the full grain in the ear." At many points the evolution of the Japanese Bible and the Constitution of Japan was parallel. It would be hard to imagine one without the other, when the details of time, within the dates 1853 and 1889, are kept in mind. Along with the intense political struggle went the quiet, but none the less earnest labors of the study.

On February 3, 1888, the church in Tokyo near the Shin Sakai Bashi, that is, the new Sakai Bridge over the Sumida River, in the foreign quarter called Tsukiji (filled up, or made land), the largest Protestant place of worship in the capital, was filled to the utmost capacity by an audience consisting of aliens and natives, but all bound together with the same ties of interest and expectation.

The Japanese and English Bibles lay on the speaker's desk — fit emblem of the true accord that — it is to be hoped — will ever be maintained between the Japanese and English-speaking people. One set of the Holy Scriptures, handsomely bound and in five volumes, had been presented on December 31, 1887, to Dr. Hepburn by the National Bible Society of Scotland. Representatives of fourteen American and English missionary societies and of the native Protestant churches in the capital were present. Dr. Hepburn, having completed sixteen years of labor in translation, was in the chair.

The exercises were opened by the venerable Bishop Williams of the American Episcopal Church, one of the first missionaries on the ground, in 1859, who read the Nineteenth Psalm in English, and this was also read by Rev. (afterwards Bishop) Y. Honda of the Methodist Church of Japan. After prayer by Rev. James Williams, of the English Church Missionary Society, a short address was made by Rev. J. T. Isé (afterwards Yokoi), a Congregational pastor. Rev. Messrs. Inagaki and Okuno also took part.

Dr. Hepburn, as chairman of the Permanent Committee appointed in 1878 to translate and publish the Bible in Japanese, then gave in detail and at length a history of the work done. After naming his foreign helpers, he paid a warm tribute to his daily companions in study, Rev. Matsuyama and Mr. Takahashi Goro. Both these Christian gentlemen, accomplished scholars in their own language, sat with the Yokohama Committee during the six years or more of work upon the New Testament. They thus received a training which made them such efficient workers in translating the Old Testament, enabling the committee to attain uniformity and agreement in the style and character of the whole book, quite equal to that of the Revised Version in English.

He called attention to the fact that the new Japanese Bible is in the pure native and simple style easily understood by the most unlearned. Being so chaste and free from Chinese and foreign terms, and read by millions of its people, it will have a powerful influence in preserving the native tongue in its purity. Undoubtedly it will do for the Japanese language much of what has been done for the tongue of England by the pure Anglo-Saxon of the English Bible.

Then he explained in some detail the method pursued by the revisers:

"Throughout the whole work the committee endeavored to adhere faithfully and as literally as possible to the Hebrew original, desiring not only to give its true meaning, but also to retain the beautiful and instructive figurative language in which God has conveyed his mind to the children of men." All scholarly aids possible were made use of, comparison being constantly made with the Revised Version of the Holy Scriptures in English. "They have had no particular difficulty in their work, except it be in finding satisfactory equivalents for some of the animals, birds, insects, trees, flowers and precious stones mentioned in the Bible; but they trust that in these respects also, they have attained to the true meaning as nearly as most of the modern versions. Instead of translating the names of the Hebrew weights, measures and months, the Hebrew terms were transferred into Japanese *kana*.

"And now, my Christian brethren, it only remains for me to take this translation of the Old Testament, the work of the Permanent Committee, united with the translation of the New Testament, the work of the Yokohama Committee, and make it into one Bible, in the name of the whole body of Protestant missionaries in Japan, and I may say of the whole Church of Christ in America and England, and offer it as a loving present to the Japanese nation."

Suiting the action to the word, Dr. Hepburn took the copy of the Old Testament in one hand and the copy of the New Testament in the other, and, reverently placing them together, laid the book — a complete Bible — upon the desk. The audience was visibly moved at this simple but significant action.

His closing sentences, eloquent, and spoken with deep feeling, carried the conviction of the speaker to other minds. "What more precious gift — more precious than mountains of silver and gold — could the Christian people of the West bestow on the people of this land? May the sacred Book be to the Japanese what it has been to the people of the West, a fountain of life, a messenger of joy and peace, the foundation of a true civilization, of social and political prosperity and greatness. May it be to them like the river, which Ezekiel saw proceeding out from the throne of God, which, wherever it flowed, brought life and healing. And shall we not now call upon our souls and all that is within us to thank our God and Father for this, his wonderful gift to the children of men, that in his loving-kindness he has sent it to this people?"

Dr. Guido F. Verbeck then spoke in Japanese, reproducing in substance what Dr. Hepburn had said.

Rev. George Cochran, D.D., the eloquent Canadian, then gave a scholarly address, outlining the work of translation and the dispersion of the Scriptures throughout the world, briefly glancing at the Septuagint, the Syriac, Latin, Coptic, Gothic, Saxon and other versions. These seemed to spread and perpetuate the knowledge of the truth during the paralysis of progress and the eclipse of faith that fell upon the Church in the medieval night of Christendom. He dwelt upon the thrill of life and the era of evangelism which sprang from the translations of the Bible into the vernacular, and how the Bible had become the people's book. He rejoiced in the organization of the Bible societies of Christendom, "that like twin sisters, fellow handmaids waiting upon our Lord, shall not rest nor be discouraged until the Word of life is in the hand of every creature upon earth. . . . In this, the highest ministry of man's good will, the English-speaking people of Britain and America unite their strength." He glanced at India and China, and then spoke of Japan — "at peace with all the world, appropriating by the swift and ready adaptation to the genius of her people, the material and intellectual civilization of the West." The plowshare of evolution had freshly turned up generous soil. "By the open furrows gathered quickly a numerous band of gospel husbandmen waiting ready to cast in the imperishable seed. The translator should put into the hand of these husbandmen the seed basket full, replenished for all time; now the laborers may broadcast the seed, the Word of God, wherever they will, and it shall surely grow. . . . Its principles of holy truth and love shall weave themselves into the thought and speech and life of each successive generation. They shall enter into the new Imperial Constitution, into the laws and customs of the land, and by virtue of their healing, quickening power, the ancient empire shall put on moral strength and may endure with vigor till the last courses of the sun."

After this eloquent apostrophe, closing with a brilliant prophecy—a Christian Banzai—there was a brief address by Mr. Inagaki, pastor of the first

(Kaigan) church formed in Japan. Then the venerable Okuno offered the closing prayer. The final, apostolical word of blessing was by Rev. Julius Soper of the Methodist Episcopal Church.

It was a high and glorious day, long to be remembered and auspicious for the good of "millions yet to be," as well as to those then living. Not least, in beauty and charm as well as in cheer and promise, was the presence of a choir of Christian girls and women from the Japanese churches of the capital. Some remembered how Townsend Harris in 1857 had held, with his secretary, Mr. Heusken, the first Christian worship in Yedo and they recalled his favorite Scripture — "What hath God wrought!"

No history of Bible translation in Japan can even approach completion that omits the name of a true yoke-fellow with Dr. Hepburn, Rev. Nathan Brown, D.D., whom I knew well and honored highly. Both were veterans who had passed through many perils.

It was good to see the two old men together. The latter lived thirty-four years in Asia, and was for seventy years a member of the Baptist Church. He translated the entire New Testament and portions of the Old Testament into two languages as different as the Assamese and Japanese. His hymns are sung in English, Assamese, Burmese and Japanese. He filled the positions of teacher, editor, preacher, naturalist and translator, besides making abundant antiquarian and philological research, passing unscathed through innumerable perils. When he died his body was carried to burial — at his own request — by devout natives of Japan, and on his tombstone was engraved, beside name and date, the prayer, "God bless the Japanese."

XVII

A SAMURAI OF JESUS

HOW God raises up particular men to do special work is strikingly illustrated in the case of Rev. Okuno Masatusuna, who gave Dr. Hepburn such valuable assistance in his work of translation. In the making of this, his child, the almighty Father produced a masterpiece. In superb physical and intellectual balance, equipped with all the learning of Japan, a scholar in Shinto, Buddhism, and the Confucian classics and philosophy, critically versed in all the forms of the language, withal a superb penman, Okuno was just the helper that Dr. Hepburn had long been seeking. Introduced to the great translator in the spring of 1871, Okuno by degrees communicated to his American friend his remarkable personal history. The story of his life opens a window into the life of Old Japan.

Okuno was a samurai of the samurai. He was born in Yedo in 1822. When he was five years old, his mother died. On account of his unyielding spirit, he was disliked by his stepmother. He left his home to live at one of the Buddhist temples in Uyéno. His threefold training was that of the Buddhist neophyte,

A DISCIPLE OF CHRIST   A DISCIPLE OF BUDDHA

OKUNO

the man at arms, and the Confucian scholar. He studied Buddhism thoroughly, learning all about its sects and its doctrinal evolutions, but he had little faith in the alleged truth of its dogmas. Giving himself to the Chinese classics, he became a master of the philosophy of China, and the doctrines of Confucius, whether in their original form; or, in their restatement, in the twelfth century, by Chu Hi; or, in that phase which re-created the mind of Japan and in which the leaders of the revolution of 1868 were trained, the Oyoméi so named after a Chinese sage and general.

Okuno's physical training was thorough. He became so skillful in the art of fencing and in spear exercise, that at eighteen, he passed a successful examination in military science and was given a special reward by his master. He was highly accomplished also in the use of the gentler arts, such as jiujitsu, or self-defense without weapons. In music, he excelled in playing the flute, so that he was often in demand at the theater and social entertainments. His desire was ever to excel, but at twenty-four he was prostrated on account of his intense application to study; so that his father took all his books away from him. He, however, secretly managed to possess himself of them again and spent many hours in reading. His bold and chivalrous spirit made him a candidate for offices of responsibility, but these brought him among wicked and dissipated companions, and he became a leader in sinful indulgences.

When the southwestern clans made a combination against the Bakufu, or shogun's government in Yedo, civil war began, lasting, off and on, four or five years, from 1863 to 1868. Okuno was in several battles and did valiant service, but, when the Yedo army was irretrievably beaten, he took refuge on board of a man-of-war, once being nearly captured by one of the imperial warships. Seeing no hope at sea, he fled to Shidzuoka and there became a page to the Prince Rinnoji, who had for a time, in 1868, been set up by interested followers as a pretender to the throne. He also acted as a messenger of the shogun Keiki, who was an exile in this "Saint Helena of Tokugawaism." When the new Imperial Government was established, Okuno was in utter despair, for all hope of reëstablishing the old regime had to be given up. He offered himself a vicarious sacrifice and was willing to die for his master. He petitioned the Imperial Government thus: "Let us endure the penalty, and let our master go free." No notice was taken of this prayer. Although not molested, Okuno was in extreme distress, having no means of support.

It was when meditating upon dying for his master, that he was met by a priest — evidently in want of money — who persuaded him to make special gifts for the restoration of his master to power. So Okuno wrote out a petition and laid it before the golden idols, of which Japan has even yet an immeasurable forest. Of its population in wood, stone and metal, gilded, lacquered, green with patina or polished by hands of prayer, no census has ever been taken, while thousands of persons still gain a living by carving these effigies, or by duping their devotees. From this time forth, Okuno gave himself to rigors which emaciated his body and saddened his soul. He fasted days at a time, bathed in ice-cold water every morning for many months, ate no rice, but only potatoes and buckwheat; and sat for long, dreary hours on coarse straw mats, keeping vigil and reciting prayers from the sacred books. All these were of no avail. Then he complained to the priest, who told him he must try some other way. If he would visit a great number of temples and make offering at each to Inari, the god of rice, his petitions for peace and prosperity would be granted.

So setting out on foot, this passionate pilgrim visited in person one thousand temples. According to the report of his proxies, he offered prayers also at no fewer than fifteen thousand other temples, making sixteen thousand petitions; for all pagans, of whatever name, think that they are heard because of their much speaking. Now surely, he thought, his prayers would be answered, but not even a sign of having been heard was vouchsafed. Infuriated at this silence on the part of the gods, Okuno, the disappointed, reproached the priest for his greed and deception, knocked over and trampled on the images once thought sacred and went back to his former habits of dissipation. He gave up all his belief in deity, or a future life. With health broken, and without money or credit, he was in utter destitution and misery.

Employment with Dr. S. R. Brown, whom he first served as a teacher and scholar, secured him food. In time, the earnest preaching of Rev. J. H. Ballagh led him to see himself as he was, before God, a needy sinner, yet hungering for pardon and righteousness. In July, 1872, at the risk of his life, and acting as bravely as when loyally fighting in the forefront for his master on the bloody field, he made a public confession of his faith and was baptized by the Rev. S. R. Brown.

His superior penmanship was greatly admired and he prepared the first edition to the New Testament, his manuscript being produced from the blocks. The men who worked for him knew that they would be imprisoned, or put to death, if spied upon and discovered.

When Mr. Loomis secured Okuno as a teacher, while Dr. Hepburn was in the United States, the American asked the Japanese, "Are you not afraid of being arrested, or punished for being a Christian and doing Christian work?" Drawing his finger significantly across his neck, he replied, "They may cut off my head, but they cannot destroy my soul." For years, there hung over every native Christian convert, as by a silken filament, the suspended sword of the executioner. I felt this when I was with them, and I never knew finer courage even in our Civil War.

God raised up Okuno to be the first poet of the

Christian Church. He was the beginner of native hymnology. A literal translation of the hymn "Jesus loves me" had been made, probably first by Rev. Jonathan Goble. The assuring sentiment, and the tune to which it was sung, made it an instant favorite with the Japanese Christians, and its traditional associations keep it popular even to this day. Nevertheless, the way in which the Mikado's vernacular was tortured, to make some distant approach to sense, reminds one of the Yiddish of Chatham Street, as compared with the classic Hebrew in Isaiah. The Japanese scholars have made merry over this blessed doggerel.

One day Okuno came to Mr. Loomis with a roll of manuscript, saying that he had sung that hymn a good while, but never before understood it. Mr. Loomis at once said, "Why not put it into rhyme and meter, so that the Japanese will understand it when they sing?" Okuno, after several days, did put it into good language, though the meter and style of the original were unknown to the older Japanese prosody. A beginning had been made, however, and, encouraged by Mr. Loomis, Okuno went on and translated about fifteen more of the most familiar modern Christian songs of praise to God, which were published with the title, "Religious Hymns."

In 1876, when a new and enlarged hymnal was issued, the Japanese Christians were delighted to find that, of the more than fifty hymns, several were Okuno's original compositions.

No sooner was Okuno a new man in Christ Jesus, than he began to tell at once of his Saviour's great love for those who were lost in sin. He besought men night and day with tears to become reconciled to God.

Thus bloomed forth, on Japanese soil, the consummate white flower of Christian loyalty. Among the rare jewels of race and civilization which have slowly grown to perfection is the Japanese virtue of loyalty. In supreme devotion, in utter consecration to his master, in service, through life and in death, a samurai's loyalty to his Lord knew no equal. Like the great "No Two Such" Mountain, Fuji San, this loyalty was high, serene and pure. Beside it no lesser mountain, no petty hill must rear its form. Wife, children, fortune, health, friends, were as naught — but rather to be trampled under foot, if necessary, in order to reach that "last supreme measure of devotion" which the samurai owed to his lord. The matchless sphere of rock crystal, flawless and perfect, is the emblem of Japanese loyalty, which, by amazing transit from what was petty and local, to a single object, the Emperor, explains the secret of the ability of the Japanese David to humble the Russian Goliath. Japanese loyalty, brought to full fruition, after a thousand years of training in the national framework, when dedicated to Jesus, creates under the Holy Spirit's promptings as noble specimens of glorious manhood as this earth or known human history has ever seen. I lived under the feudal system in Old Japan and knew the first Christian samurai, and I testify to what I have seen.

Such a consummate spirit was Okuno. He was a preacher of rare and winning power. When I first heard him — being able, after a year's exile in the interior, to understand most of his discourse — he seemed to me an incarnate day of Pentecost. Preaching on the Prodigal Son, to his rapt countrymen, and using a language which aliens had declared unfitted by its crass earthiness to hold the heavenly treasure, he marked a distinct epoch in the history of Japan. I listened to torrents of eloquence. I was led into vast chambers of imagery. I was melted by tenderness of appeal, that bore me in imagination to angelic realms, until I felt no longer on earth, but amid the choirs of heaven.

Okuno's heart was set upon giving to his people a knowledge of the true God, and he was never satisfied to allow surcease to his labors, until he had toured in almost every province in the empire, preaching the good news of God. Then the failure of his bodily strength compelled him to halt.

He was never content with repeating old discourses or resting on laurels already won, but was always in quest of fresh seed thought. When a missionary suggested to him some appropriate text, told some telling illustration, or uttered a kindling thought, Okuno's joy was like that of a child at receiving a gift. Then his face beamed with joy that made

[175]

one, on seeing it, believe in the immortality of the soul. To preach Christ was his greatest delight.

For years, as translator, he devoted himself body and soul to the joyful work. Then he became pastor of Christian churches at Yokosuka, living under the shadow of Will Adams' grave, and at Osaka, and other places. On special occasions, he was in demand, his addresses being strikingly happy and often eloquent. He started on his third and final evangelistic tour in southern Japan, April 4, 1903. As he grew older, he seemed to be more active. At seventy, he was so full of fire and energy that he wanted to go over all Japan again to preach, but he had to give up the idea. It was estimated that he had already preached over four thousand sermons and was in every way acknowledged as one of the great leaders in the conquest of Japan for that Master before whom all other masters are to be put as names and shadows.

In later years, "Father Okuno" was his title, for, as has been well said, "While exceptional intellectual abilities will command regard during youth, it is only exceptional spiritual attainment that will command regard when one has become advanced in years," and Okuno won all hearts by his humility and piety.

XVIII

THE STORY OF THE CHURCHES

WHILE in Japan, during the war between the States in America, Dr. Hepburn was truly loyal both to the government and to the Northern Church, under both of which he had been born and nurtured. It was during the first half of this period of anxiety that Americans abroad felt as though they had no country, for our commerce had been swept off the seas, and letters home had to be sent by way of Great Britain. Rev. Leighton Wilson, secretary of the Southern Presbyterian Board, had importuned him to represent them in China — and the Doctor had a southern wife; but in this matter, as in other subjects, he was very quiet and firm in his convictions. At the outset, he was hardly reconciled, as we shall see, even to the union of the Reformed and Presbyterian mission in a single organization.

It is now time to tell of the growth of the native Christian community into a church. Rev. James H. Ballagh, of the Reformed Church in America, and the first young missionary in Japan, had arrived at Yokohama, November 7, 1861. He had rapidly gained mastery of the colloquial, so that "the common people heard him gladly." He excelled as a preacher, and won converts. He was the first pastor in eastern Japan, and he built a small stone chapel on the lot secured by the missionaries — about which hangs many a tale.

Much difficulty was experienced in getting a title to land in the new settlement (while Kanagawa was still technically by treaty the real place promised by the Japanese), and the matter was delayed until 1864, when the deed was obtained and transferred to the Missionary Board. In the great fire of November 25, 1866, the lot in question was swept by the flames. Then, in order to hold it as church property, Mr. Ballagh erected a little edifice, often called "the first church in Japan," which is now a chapel attached to the Kaigan church which, in 1911, celebrated the jubilee of the arrival of Mr. Ballagh, who still, in 1913, toils on, though over eighty years of age. It was a small building of stone, pretty enough in its way, but it gave the ungodly, the joke-makers, the "globe trotters," the thoughtless, and especially the malicious liers in wait for scandal, their opportunity. A petty war of jibes and caricatures began. Even salaried officers of the U. S. Government took it upon themselves to photograph the pygmy building in juxtaposition with one much larger, that it might stand as a dwarf beside a mighty architectural giant, of which the next paragraph tells.

While Mr. Ballagh was in America, the Rev.

David Thompson of the Presbyterian Church, North, who arrived May 18, 1863, and who held the power of attorney, arranged for a handsome two-story dwelling house to be built for Messrs. Burgess and Burdick on the lot adjoining. This was rented for several years, and afterwards was bought, for only two thousand dollars, because of value received in the way of rent, and duly transferred to the Mission Board. The photographers and jokesmiths became even more industrious and disseminated their funny pictures over the world. Under the large and handsome building was inscribed "Mr. Ballagh's residence, $4,000"; while over the little chapel was the legend "Of the few remaining bricks, for the Lord, $600."

The facts were afterwards investigated by the United States authorities and the official person chiefly responsible for the libel was superseded. Students of missionary history know that a similar story — the egg of the fowl hatched in Japan — started in India, probably before Mr. Ballagh was born, and began an eastward journey, doing service at Calcutta, Singapore, Shanghai, and other places before reaching the Mikado's empire. "Nothing travels faster than a lively story." Mark Twain said that there were only twenty-three original jokes.

On November 5, 1865, Dr. Hepburn wrote: "I accompanied Rev. James Ballagh, who baptized Mr. Yano Riuzan, who had been a teacher of Rev. S. R. Brown. He was the first convert to the gospel in eastern Japan." Others were won to the Master through the preaching and teaching, and on March 10, 1872, the first Church of Christ in Japan was formed, with eleven members. This Yokohama church was without the name of, or connection with, any denomination.

For the large edifice of this "Kaigan" or Seashore Church, Hon. Townsend Harris, the United States Minister, contributed $1,000; an English merchant and the Sandwich Island Christians, $1,000; Hon. Robert H. Pruyn, Mr. Harris' successor, $500. Mr. Ballagh collected $2,500 in America. The structure, occupying part of the Perry Treaty ground of 1854, was dedicated July 10, 1875. It is still standing (1913), the church having more than four hundred members.

The Union Church, made up of foreign residents and now flourishing, with a settled pastor, had also a history through evolution.

When conducting public worship in the early sixties, as so many English people were present, Dr. S. R. Brown officiated according to the forms of the Church of England, until, in July, 1862, Mr. Bailey, English chaplain, arrived. In February, 1863, several gentlemen, who preferred a simpler form of divine service, met at the house of the United States consul at Kanawaga, and effected an organization in connection with the (Dutch) Reformed Church in America — which enjoys also the honor of having the first fully organized Protestant church on the

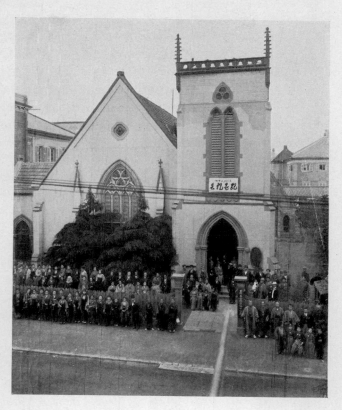

UNION CHURCH AT YOKAHOMA
Organized 1868

continent of America, the date of the organization being 1628. This Union congregation in Yokohama worshiped first in the Masonic lodge room and later in Dr. Hepburn's dispensary, until 1868, when the present Union Church was organized.

Rev. C. Carrothers and his wife, of the Presbyterian Church, North, and Rev. O. M. Greene arrived in Japan in 1869 and Rev. Mr. and Mrs. Cornes and Rev. David Thompson established a station in Tokyo. Rev. Henry and Mrs. Loomis and Rev. E. Rothesay Miller joined the mission in 1872, in which year also the Woman's societies entered the field, represented by the Misses Youngman and Gamble. In 1873 two native churches were formed, one at the port and the other in the capital; that in Tokyo being organized on September 25, 1873.

On December 30, 1873, the six Presbyterian brethren, by order of the General Assembly, formed a presbytery and organized a church; but against this, David Thompson of the same mission and Mr. Ballagh of the Reformed Church remonstrated. To them, Dr. Hepburn replied, "It is impossible on earth for a church union; it might be in heaven." Thus matters went on, the church in Tsukiji, Tokyo, with Dr. Thompson, and the Kaigan church in Yokohama, with Mr. Ballagh, forming The Church of Christ in Japan, while the native church, with Messrs. Carrothers and Greene, was known as the Presbyterian Church. This continued till the arrival, in 1875, of Rev. William Imbrie to join the Presbyterian Mission, as his cousin, Rev. E. R. Miller, had done two or three years before him. Mr. Miller, seeing the trend of things, and having married Miss M. E. Kidder of the Reformed Mission, by consent of his Board transferred his connection to the Reformed Church Mission. Dr. Thompson had also resigned from his mission, and had accepted the position of interpreter to the American Legation, though carrying on his pastoral work with the Tsukiji church and aiding it financially. In 1877, all the churches holding to the order of government by elders, or the Presbyterian and Reformed Church, united in one federation or union under the name of the United Church of Christ in Japan. In 1890 they dropped the word "united" and adopted as their Confession of Faith the Apostles' Creed, with a simple doctrinal preface.

XIX

TWO NOBLE MONUMENTS

DURING the year 1872 Dr. and Mrs. Hepburn made a voyage home by way of the Suez canal. While in America, the Doctor secured from his friends a handsome sum of money for the building of the Shiloh church edifice in Yokohama, to which he was to give many years of loving service.

A chapter must be devoted to this church and to the Méiji Gaku-in, or (academic and theological) College of the Era of Méiji, in Tokyo. Perhaps the best translation of "Méiji" would be Enlightened Rule (or Government). The Hebrew term *Mishpat*, translated "Judgment" in our Bible, does perhaps express more fully the ideas which the Japanese comprehend under the idea of "government" and we under the term "civilization."

The elegant new church edifice in Onoé Cho, (street at the end of the Inlet) near the railway station, which was dedicated in January, 1892, had been upwards of a year in building. The gift of personal friends of Dr. Hepburn, it is, without exception, the finest church in Yokohama, having been constructed of the most substantial materials. Brick, with stone trimmings, was used and the finish of both exterior and interior reflects great credit on the architect, Mr. Sarda. The audience room has two entrances, through the two towers, with a lecture or Sunday-school room attached, while the equipment, of circular seats, electric lights and heating arrangements, is most complete.

The historical paper read at the dedication showed that "The body of Christians, for whose use this building was erected, began organized existence in what was for years Dr. Hepburn's dispensary. Thence they moved to a large wooden building erected for their use in Sumiyoshi Cho. At this time, the membership numbered three hundred, the pastor being the Rev. Hidétaro Yamamoto."

The dedicatory services were in Japanese; Mr. Okuno reading the Scriptures, Dr. Imbrie delivering the sermon, and Dr. David Thompson offering the dedicatory prayer. Mr. Nishimura, an efficient elder of the church, was at the organ.

A collation was afterwards served to foreign and native guests. At the end of the room were set life-size crayon sketches of Dr. and Mrs. Hepburn, which were to adorn the pastor's study. These were the work of Professor S. Hayashi. A room in one of the towers was to be used for prayer circles or private conference, and another, of similar size, in the other tower, was for the pastor.

Dr. Hepburn's letter, committing the sacred edifice to their care, reads as follows:

THE MÉIJI GAKU-IN AND CHAPEL

TWO NOBLE MONUMENTS

To the pastors, elders and members of the Shiloh church:

MY DEAR BRETHREN:

In taking leave of you and handing over this church to your care, I desire to say that I have endeavored faithfully to employ the funds and fulfill the intentions of the many Christian friends who have so liberally and unitedly contributed to the building. In erecting this church and presenting it to you, we desire to afford you a place for the worship of God and our Saviour Jesus Christ, and from which should ever be proclaimed the knowledge of God and that great salvation through our Lord Jesus Christ, which he has provided for all men. It is our earnest desire, dear friends, that you be always careful to keep it only for this purpose, and not profane it by using it for any secular purpose whatever, or for any meeting that has not the honor of God and the moral interest of men in view.

Dr. Hepburn built a house on a portion of the ground belonging to the Méiji Gaku-in, Mr. McNair being the architect. In this he had expected to reside; but later, concluding not to remove from Yokohama, he presented the building to the Presbyterian Board of Foreign Missions. By a vote of the standing committee, held on July 3, 1888, the house was received and a resolution of thanks adopted.

Dr. Hepburn resigned the presidency of the Méiji Gaku-in, and his resignation was accepted by the directors, October 13, 1892. The document was signed by Rev. George William Knox and Naomi Tamura.

One of the most interesting services was that of the synod of the Church of Christ in Japan. After important business, the members assembled in the chapel of Sandham Hall, to witness the inauguration of the Rev. K. Ibuka, A.M., as president of the Méiji Gaku-in, in succession to Dr. Hepburn. Addresses were made by the two presidents, by Dr. G. F. Verbeck and by Prof. M. N. Wyckoff, of the Reformed Church in America, besides Messrs. Inagaki and Uyémura. Flags, flowers and the Bible were in notable evidence. The organ gave forth the music of "Coronation," "Ward" and "Old Hundred."

After prayer by Rev. Isagawa, the Forty-eighth Psalm was read by Mr. Ogawa, the oldest Christian pastor in Tokyo. Dr. Hepburn, in giving its history, spoke of the very small beginning, from an elementary day school for teaching English in Yokohama, and the various stages of progress until now, when it was to be put mainly under the management and instruction of educated and competent Japanese — the goal which foreign teachers have ever aimed at and hoped to reach in their work.

One can imagine the pleasing smile on the face of the Doctor, when he welcomed Mr. Ibuka, and said:

"May we not regard his name as auspicious, as a presage of future good to the college, that as Ibuka — a well deep with pure and living water — he may diffuse a refreshing and healthful influence all around; and as Kajinosuké, my successor at the helm of this noble institution, the Méiji Gaku-in, he may always steer it on a safe and prosperous course, avoiding all the dangerous rocks and shoals that may be in his way."

The applause following this bright, witty and appropriate speech was vigorous.

President Ibuka's address in Japanese, equally modest and beautiful, followed. He reviewed Dr. Hepburn's labors and the work of education in Japan and foreshadowed the future of the work which he hoped the institution was to carry on.

When Verbeck, the eloquent, spoke, he captivated the audience by his fluent and logical discourse, seasoned with many a sparkling and witty thrust at smatterers, whether in theology, science, or other departments of life. He laid emphasis on what constituted the source of Christianity. It was the doctrine or teachings of Christ. He showed the need of systematic teaching, which was as necessary as maps and charts to the navigator. Creed and confessions were requisite for preventing errors, as well as for making strong and perfectly formed Christian men. As water never rose higher than its source, so no man lived above his creed. Fortunately creeds do neither make nor alter the truth of Christianity any more than the system of astronomy creates the laws of the heavenly bodies. He congratulated all upon the choice of the new president.

At the end of the sessions of the synod, after communion of the Lord's Supper had been enjoyed, the evidences of their environment, in the archipelago, which is so geologically young, were strikingly manifested in the resolutions of sympathy with the sufferers from natural calamities. I. Oishi, who, with his wife had been killed in the recent Nagoya earthquake, was a member of the synod of the previous year.

An address, November 8, 1892, from the Japanese churches of Osaka to Dr. Hepburn, contained many touching sentences. This letter was in the name of the synod of the Church of Christ in Japan, then in session at Osaka.

"It is now thirty-three years ago — when Japan was but one of the darkest spots on the globe — that you landed on our then unwelcome shores." The Doctor was congratulated as a pioneer and as a physician — "the father of medical science in this part of Asia." As a lexicographer, "he saved thousands of students, both natives and foreigners, toils and discouragements, that might have resulted in despair." As a translator, "he left the people a perpetual blessing — that of reading the Word of God in their own tongue." As president of the Méiji Gaku-in, direct worker in the vineyard of the Lord, he saw the completion of the Shiloh church. The letter ended with blessings, good wishes and prayers. It was signed by the president, Mr. Ohgimi, and the secretary, Mr. Yamamoto.

XX

FAREWELL TO JAPAN

W HEN the Hepburns were about to leave their island home, there was no end to the expressions of regard from the people. They looked upon this old couple who — for over a half century, thirty-three years of which had been spent in Japan — had walked hand and hand together along life's pathway, as embodying both the Christian and the marital ideal. The contrast between the hermit land of 1859 and the empire of 1892 lent many a suggestion to the occasion. In this chapter is condensed the substance of the addresses of many speakers, as they uttered their sad, grateful, *sayonara*, or farewell.

One native orator named two institutions as growing almost directly out of the work of this couple, one being the Ferris Seminary, or School for Girls, of the Reformed Church in America, situated on the Bluff in Yokohama, which grew out of the work of Mrs. Hepburn; and the Méiji Gaku-in, or College and Theological School which developed from the Doctor's labors. These, with the dictionary and the translation of the Bible, made four great monuments.

The prejudices of the insulars against the outsiders in old days seemed once, like that of the cities of the plain to the Israelites, "fortified up to heaven." It was the Doctor's business to break these down and to introduce the *Mishpat,* or "Judgment" of the brotherhood of the Christian world, in place of the local gods and their abominations. He had come to be a transformer of Japan.

It was the daily lives of Dr. Hepburn and his fellow workers in the early days, which wooed Japan first to tolerate and then to welcome missionaries to these shores. It is to them that Japan owes the greater part of her present advancement. "The missionary body has been Japan's chief instructor, exerting an influence wholly for enlightenment and good."

Farewell services, held at the Shiloh church, on Saturday, October 13, were attended by many native Christians, from several churches. Prayer was offered by Rev. A. Hattori of Tokyo, once a pupil of Dr. Hepburn. Okuno read, from Acts, chapter 20, Paul's farewell to the Ephesian elders.

Just as the Doctor was rising to reply to the addresses of the native pastors, a photographer asked for a moment's pause that he might take a picture. The Doctor and his wife, standing arm in arm, in the pulpit and surrounded by hundreds of their admiring children in the faith were pictured and printed by the sunlight.

It is interesting to note that photography was first introduced into Japan by Rev. Dr. S. R. Brown, who taught a Japanese, who became skillful and famous. From the Reformed, now Congregational, church in Ithaca, New York, came most of the money for this photographic equipment.

Dr. Hepburn's address in Japanese was a model of simplicity and sincerity. He recounted how sixty years ago, when first he gave his heart to Christ, he covenanted to go wherever Christ wanted him. As a servant of Jesus, he was a debtor unto all men, and in coming to Japan he only did what was his duty to do.

As the oldest resident in Yokohama — then, in 1892, a city of one hundred and fifty thousand people, — he remembered that it was in 1859 a mere fishing village, consisting of a few small huts, on a narrow strip of land surrounded by marshes. Fishing boats were out on the water, over what now constitutes the greater part of the city. He did service with a friend then, acting as a mayor, in laying out the town. The creek did not then exist, but was cut through later for purposes of isolation, or protection. The new settlement was to be a sort of Déshima, which to the Japanese was the model for the treatment of foreigners. Only a few settlers had come over from China to open business.

Professor Ishimoto rendered the Doctor's address into Japanese and this was followed by Rev. A. Hattori, in an eloquent expression of thanks to Mrs. Hepburn for the early and active part she had taken in woman's education. He said that the very first recognition of woman's work by the government, through the Department of Education, was in engaging a pupil of Mrs. Hepburn to assist Miss Margaret C. Griffis and Mrs. Peter Veeder, in the first school established in Tokyo. This afterwards led to the Normal School, while the present prosperous Reformed Church school, the Ferris Seminary on the Bluff, owed its origin to a class of pupils, which Mrs. Hepburn had turned over to Miss Mary E. Kidder [later Mrs. E. Rothesay Miller] of the Reformed Church.

An original poem by Okuno, the hymnologist, concluded the exercises. The aged poet's beautiful and sympathetic utterances and their mournful and pathetic cadences bowed the heads and suffused the eyes of the native part of his audience. It was a touching tribute of the deep affection and warm heart of the native brethren for their beloved teachers.

Then the poet became the petitioner at the throne of grace, white-haired Okuno praying for God's blessing upon the Hepburns, and upon their labors, and especially on the copy of Scriptures, presented some years before, to His Majesty, the Emperor.

The faculty and students of the Méiji College could not let Dr. Hepburn off without a farewell meeting, which was held on October 18. The city itself was on this day gay with the national flags, flying out in honor of the feast of first fruits, or the initial eating of the autumn's new rice. Over Sandham Hall, in the chapel where the services were held, there was a massive evergreen arch. The hall was filled chiefly

[192]

by students, native pastors and prominent Christian people. President Ibuka presided and Dr. Verbeck made the first address in English. He recounted the Doctor's labors in so many forms, showing especially how visible to all his work was. There was the Bible in Japanese, the great dictionary, Bible dictionary, Hepburn Hall, Shiloh church, the healing of hundreds, and more, which "could not be included in a ticket across the Pacific. . . . His life's work is efficiently, successfully, yea, well done. Everything that Dr. Hepburn put his hand to was well finished."

Dr. McAuley, representing the academic faculty, also spoke. He said that he regarded God's providence, in fitting men for their social mission, as not confined to the early ages of the Christian Church. He added the fact that about one hundred full graduates, and fifteen hundred students, who had, at one time or another, received instruction, was the record of Méiji College. Other speakers took part and then the English hymn, "Blest be the tie that binds," was sung.

Dr. Hepburn briefly replied and a touching prayer was offered by Rev. Y. Ogawa, one of the oldest Christians and Bible translators [for a few months, at first] and the first ordained minister in Japan.

Rev., now President, T. Harada, of the Doshisha University in Kyoto, represented the Congregational and other churches of Japan, in expressing their sense of indebtedness. Having never before had the pleasure of seeing or meeting the guest of the day, he told how he first came to hear the names of Hepburn. A certain eyewash had been recommended as having been a prescription of Dr. Hepburn. He obtained some and found it efficacious. Next, when a student of English and looking up the English equivalents of Japanese words, the Doctor's dictionary was of the greatest service. When he became a Christian and read the Scriptures in his mother-tongue, he learned more fully what this medical and literary missionary had done, not only for Japan but for all her people. He enlarged upon the wide scope of his influence, in Japan and also in the pupils sent abroad, who received posts of honor on their return. Many individuals and agencies had united to advance his nation, "but if one alone were to be singled out, there could be no doubt that name would be Dr. Hepburn's. . . . The proverb 'Many begin, but few end' found in him a favorable fulfillment."

The foreign residents and the Union Church people of Yokohama could not allow the aged couple to leave Japan without showing their appreciation of them. So at the Van Schaick Hall, in Ferris Seminary they gathered together on the evening of October 18, amid greenery and flowers, music and rejoicing. A. J. Wilkins, whom one might call the senior citizen in Yokohama, being called to the chair, spoke words of welcome and eulogy, remarking:

"And when I say 'they' I do not separate wife

from husband. . . . She is the secret supply of oil which feeds the flame. . . . The dictionary, evolved from chaos, after more than nine years of patient work, was an invaluable boon to merchants, and students, as well as to missionaries. His work in the dispensary was a large means of securing recognition of the value of Western science."

The British consul, Mr. Troup, also spoke feelingly. "On the one hand, the powers of the Western nations were being exhibited by force, on the other the moral ideas represented by the gospel of peace were being quietly exhibited by the Doctor's ministrations to the bodies and souls of the people."

Dr. J. H. Ballagh, besides a short speech, read a poem. Dr. Thwing spoke of the monumental service of the Doctor and of the interminable fertility of his noble, unselfish life. Dr. Meacham, pastor of the Union Church, spoke feelingly, quoting also Robert Browning's matchless verse:

> Grow old along with me!
> The best is yet to be,
> The last of life, for which the first was made:
> Our times are in His hand
> Who saith " A whole I planned,
> Youth shows but half; trust God: see all nor be afraid!"

Dr. Hepburn, rising to reply, said, "Our dear Christian friends, you have made it very hard for us to leave Japan." Then he spoke of the many men whom he had known in the East, before the Opium War of 1842 — Gutzlaff, Morrison, Williams, Medhurst, Milne, Dyer, Bridgeman — all now gone.

"One peculiarity of the Christian and foreign community at Yokohama," he said, "was that they were all as members of one family, rather like children away from home at school, each one of whom looked forward to returning home, and if one dropped out of his place he would be missed."

"The Japan Mail," which contained a notice of this farewell meeting, remarked editorially:

"To a man whose name will be remembered with respect and affection so long as Yokohama has any annals . . . the public's feeling of love and reverence . . . has constantly increased. No single person has done so much to bring foreigners and Japanese into close intercourse. . . . Hepburn's dictionary was the first book that gave access to the language of the country and remains to this day the best available interpreter of that language. . . . His life has existed to break down the old barriers of racial prejudice and distrust. . . . To the great mass of humanity a picture appeals more swiftly and remains longer and more clearly in the mind than words or writing, and to the Japanese people there is one indelible picture, the elements of which are the beauty of his character, his untiring charity and his steady zeal in the cause of everything good. . . . Happy are they who discover early in life that the best rewards of life are not in money or worldly goods. His benevolence, although always large and sometimes even trespassing on the limits of his means, was so unostentatious that few have suspected its extent. The whole of the sum gained by the sale of the second [third?] edition of his dictionary, amounting to several thousands of dollars, was devoted to the building of a spacious addition to the Méiji Gaku-in.

"Dr. Hepburn won the love of all nationalities in the settlement. He worked entirely for the good to be wrought and not for the praise to be won."

On October 18, 1892, the native doctors of Yokohama, fifty or more, many of them former pupils of Dr. Hepburn, gave him an entertainment in a Japanese restaurant, situated in a street fitly named Sumiyoshi. The name Sumiyoshi is associated in all Japanese minds with the loving old couple, who stand in the sentimental world as the representatives of happy married life and serene longevity. Besides the addresses, there were choice presents given, as souvenirs of grateful appreciation.

In the same week, a most enjoyable dinner was given in Tokyo, as a farewell, at the residence of Dr. and Mrs. David Thompson, at which nearly all the members of the East Japan Presbyterian Mission, — which Dr. Hepburn had the pleasure of establishing, a third of a century before — were present.

The Hepburns sailed for San Francisco in the steamship *Gaelic*, October 22, 1892. Even after they had gone, the stream of eulogy ceased not to flow. Two native Christian journals in Tokyo had previously contained articles on Dr. Hepburn's departure and summarized graphically in detail his scientific, medical, literary and religious work. "A

new era," wrote Professor Ishimoto in "The Evangelist," of October 7, 1892, "opened in Dr. Hepburn's
life, when he closed his dispensary and devoted himself
wholly to Bible translation. . . . Diplomatic corre-
spondence, business letters, the evangelistic work of
missionaries, and the progress of students, all owe very
much to Dr. Hepburn's dictionary. . . . Bible translation was the work of many, but the chief worker was
Dr. Hepburn. . . . The gift of the five-storied dormitory, named Hepburn Hall by the faculty, was a
notable monument of his generosity."

In "The Christian," of October 4, 1892, the situation in 1859 was pictured. Then the principle of
opening Japan to foreigners was not settled, and
the foundations of New Japan were not yet laid.
"When it was common for the patriot to take his
sword in his hand, there was a man who came to our
country with the gospel of peace. . . . The once
young and able couple have now become the old,
white-haired couple. . . . The gift which the Doctor
has made to our countrymen is his personality, more
than his work. . . . Isaiah of old described the ideal
missionary and said: 'Behold my servant . . . mine
elect. . . . I have put my Spirit upon him; he
shall bring forth judgment to the Gentiles. He
shall not cry, nor lift up, nor cause his voice to be
heard in the street.' . . . Admiring his high and pure
personality, we say of Dr. Hepburn that he is dead
to this world and his life is hid with Christ in God."

XXI

REST AFTER TOIL

A T twenty-six, Dr. Hepburn began work in the Malay world, at Singapore. At twenty-eight, he was in China. At forty-four he began the chief labors of his life in Japan. At seventy-seven, he came home for rest, little thinking, and less knowing, that twenty years of life yet awaited him.

From his last journals, as far as possible, let the Doctor tell the story of his life of quiet repose at East Orange, New Jersey.

On October 23, 1892, he made this entry: "Left Japan for the United States, not expecting to return, in the steamship *Gaelic*, and arrived in San Francisco, November 10. Went down to Pasadena, California, where we spent the winter until May 4, when we started for New York by the Southern Pacific Railway, stopping at several places on the way, arriving in New York on May 19. Going to East Orange on May 24, we remained with Dr. Lowrie, until Monday, May 29, when we took possession of the house, No. 384 Williams Street."

On July 6 he purchased the house and lot No. 71 Glenwood Avenue. Ah! how the Doctor and his wife did miss the good servants, the universal politeness, the lovely scenery of Japan! Let the veil be drawn over some of the first housekeeping experiences with "help" in East Orange!

On November 27, Dr. Hepburn was elected an elder of the Brick Presbyterian Church at East Orange, and was installed on December 30. For years he enjoyed his service.

Always sensitive to changing temperature, in his journals he kept records of heat and cold from his early life to his eventide. It is amusing to think of the vast contrast between his almost changeless temper — which resembled an ocean in calm, or a spirit level with the bubble always in the center — and the great cosmic air-ocean, which, never at rest, was continually churned by winds, moved by the sun's heat and the night's cold, and often heaving with storms.

With him, the idea and practice of a journal was a record of temperatures, varied with a minute and accurate note of the particular chapter or verse he was translating, of the line or page of the dictionary he was making or revising — he made no ineffectual notes, they were all useful. Emotions usually found expression in prayer or accompanied brief notices of events or persons. Tender, wise, or philosophic, they savored of sincere piety.

On June 17, 1897, he made an entry which calls up amusing associations to those who knew the Doctor and his tendency to take literally the words of

DR. HEPBURN
At 78 years
Taken soon after his return to America from Japan

Jesus, "sell all . . . and . . . follow me." It is this: "Deposited a trunk, containing a silver tea set, in the safe of the People's Bank." Behind this sentence-record, lies a history. That elegant silver tea service was the gift of the merchants of Yokohama to Dr. Hepburn, presented to him when he was about to leave Japan for America. He had been so long a friend of everybody, and had won, as few missionaries do, or can, the love and regard of all classes, including the commercial body in Yokohama, that they quietly collected a large sum of money and invested it in a silver tea service, made in Japan. This was duly presented to him, but, with the proviso, which was "nominated in the bond" and signed by the Doctor himself, that he would never sell it for any religious or philanthropic purpose, or for any object outside of his immediate personal advantage. His friends had a merry laugh about this. Then, in East Orange, probably to afford no temptation, either to burglars or to himself, he put it in the safety vault of the bank!

The Doctor had so great an aversion to laying up treasures upon earth — having so keen a vision of the true riches — that the very furnishing of his house seemed more Japanese than American. It was certainly a home of appalling simplicity in the eyes of some ostentatious persons in Uncle Sam's country, whose one great desire was to show off dress, pelf, upholstery, cabinet ware and china. The Doctor was not the only one, in the Land of the

Almighty Dollar, to confess gladly his purification
of taste and love of the chastely simple, because of
long residence in Japan. The æsthetic Japanese
have a dislike of display, and "a horror of the too
much," that is truly Grecian. Hundreds of Americans gladly confess their debt, in æsthetic instruction,
to the Japanese. It is certain that the Doctor, content with such things as barely ministered to his comfort, was supremely happy in enjoying the Invisible.
It was a means of grace for him to look into the
average shop window on Broadway and see how
many things there were in this world which he did
not want.

On January 21, 1895, he went to Campbell Hall,
New York, to celebrate the fiftieth anniversary of
his brother Slaytor's ordination to the ministry. Two
months later, this brother passed away. When apparently in good health, he was smitten with paralysis, and after a week's unconsciousness died, and was
buried at East Orange. "Thus suddenly, and without warning, passed away one of God's faithful
servants from this earth to wake up in heaven."
On May 30, the widow of his brother Slaytor died of
pneumonia; and on November 15, another relative,
Samuel Hepburn, of Carlisle, Pennsylvania, aged
ninety-one, died. The Doctor's life was becoming
increasingly lonely.

On March 23, 1895, the Hepburns attended the
twenty-fifth anniversary of the Woman's Foreign
Missionary Society in Philadelphia. A great and

noble movement, out of the heart of American Christian womanhood, in behalf of Asia and of all humanity had come to maturity, the grand results justifying the organization and crowning its work.

At another time, we find the Hepburns going to Princeton to attend the funeral of Mr. Ichimoto. A few days afterwards, Mrs. Keswick, daughter of Sir Harry Parkes, the indomitably active plenipotentiary of Great Britain for so many years in Japan and China, called on the Hepburns. She was on her way to England from Japan. One of the Doctor's warm friendships had been with Sir Harry, who was a nephew of Rev. Karl Gutzlaff.

On March 30, 1901, the Doctor wrote me that he was in very good health, with no evidence of disease of any kind in his body, but only a general feeling of weariness. He was easily tired and had "a slight soreness of feet, due to an attack of gout, some twenty years ago," which disabled him from taking long walks.

He wrote further: "I may say that I have no objection to your receiving and making use of all such papers and journals of mine, after my decease, as you may consider useful in the history [of the American Makers of the New Japan] which you contemplate, if you think, after full and serious consideration, it would be worth while or desirable.

"As for myself, I have not a spark of ambition or desire that any more notice of my life or work should be made public than has naturally been through missionary journals, and I hope you may come to the same conclusion. I will leave it to your own judgment, after you have thought it over.

"In judging of my own character and abilities, I may say that I am only a plodder, of average talents, and of plain common sense; if remarkable for anything, it has been for industry and perseverance, working steadily on one line and toward one object. I have been studious, rather retiring and unsocial, and of sedentary habit, without much force, vigor, or activity. Have been subject to such trials, temptations and difficulties as are common to man, and, leaning on the arm of God, have nearly reached the end of my long journey.

"I may say that the Father has been very kind and very dear to me, granting me and my dear wife such long lives, so comfortable and free from worldly cares."

He believed in keeping nothing in his own hands, when what he had to offer could be of more service elsewhere. On May 7, 1902, the Board of Foreign Missions of the Presbyterian Church passed a vote of thanks for the gift of books from Dr. Hepburn's library, consisting mostly of the Transactions of the Asiatic Society of Japan, and of the Japan Society of London — books whose value increases year by year.

He was present, on October 25, 1902, at the induction into office of Woodrow Wilson, LL.D., as president of Princeton University.

At the first banquet of the Princeton Alumni

Association of "the Oranges" — charming towns in Northern New Jersey — on the evening of November 10, there were graduates present, all the way from 1832 to 1904, the oldest and foremost being Dr. Hepburn, who said grace, after which there was a "locomotive" or train of cheers for him.

Before the great deep shadow of mental disorder, soon to fall on her — which happily did not last long, before He who "giveth his beloved sleep" called her to higher service above — Mrs. Hepburn also enjoyed a great social honor from a troop of friends. On her eighty-third birthday, when at the "Grand View Sanitarium," near Wernersville, Pennsylvania, Mrs. Hepburn was treated to a delightful surprise. Into the decorated hall of the solarium, she was brought to receive her friends. The American flag was draped over the doorway. The piano and mantel, covered with maidenhair fern and nasturtiums and plenty of palms and potted plants in view, made a bower, in which the lady of honor, seated in her chair, was the center of attention. "The young and girlish woman enjoyed the fun herself, as she was presented with a cut-glass vase, a bouquet of roses and an artistically iced cake, bearing the inscription '83 years.'" Joseph Culvert of Philadelphia read a poem, one stanza of which is as follows:

Flakes of fallen snow, that lie in clusters o'er thy brow,
Suggest of many a wintry storm since morning dawned and now,
Though still the sun's aslant the west, its setting rays impart
A glow that shows there still remains a green and sunny heart.

Her husband, entering at this moment, spoke and in a touching and eloquent manner referred to the love and devotion of his helpmate during more than sixty years of wedded life.

These were the "clouds that gather round the setting sun" — rich in lovely tints, but the prelude to twilight and night.

On December 22, 1904, the Doctor wrote me: "My heart is full of sorrow, on account of my dear wife, whom I have been compelled to send to an asylum, on account of mental derangement. This has been coming on her for several years, very gradually, until it became so violent we could not live together. She is now at a sanatorium near Paterson, New Jersey." He said he was living alone in the house with only a servant, and was sending for his only son, then in Japan, to come and take care of him.

Soon afterwards he wrote that, though feeble and in his ninetieth year, he was in excellent health. He added: "The twelfth chapter of the Epistles to the Hebrews has been a great comfort to me. Indeed, the Bible has been the greatest pleasure of my life."

Mrs. Hepburn soon passed from earth into life everlasting. Then, like a flower, bursting from the closed buds into a glory of bloom, the memory of her blossomed again in Japan, diffusing the sweet perfume to the souls of many. When news was received of her passing away, services were at once held there in memoriam, in the Shiloh church. The girls of the Union Mission School assisted in the singing, and the Ninetieth Psalm, for many years a favorite Scripture of hers, was read. The story of her life was told from various points of view by several of the leading Japanese pastors who were present. The beautiful white magnolias used in decorating the church had been arranged under the direction of Mrs. Lowder, daughter of Dr. S. R. Brown. They were taken from the garden on the Bluff belonging to Mr. Samuel D. Hepburn, the only surviving child, soon to go to America to comfort his father's remaining years. Many prominent foreign residents were seen in the audience.

The Japanese remember those who love them. One of their poets sings:

I have forgotten to forget.

XXII

MULTIPLIED HONORS

IT pleased the almighty Father to give his obedient, loving child a great surprise by permitting him to see his ninetieth birthday — something he had never expected. On this day,

> "That which should accompany old age,
> As honor, love, obedience, troops of friends"

were on hand, until his seemed

> "An old age serene and bright,
> And lovely as a Lapland night."

Yet all these were leading him — not "to the grave," but to longer life.

The first drops in the rain of honor came from Japan. It was as much for the gratification of his subjects as for his own pleasure, that Mutsuhito the Great, Emperor of Japan, conferred upon Dr. Hepburn "The Third Order of Merit of the Rising Sun, for services to spiritual and educational causes in Japan." His ambassador in Washington, Mr. Takahira, called in person upon the recipient, at East Orange, to present the diploma and insignia. It was this act that gave so much delight to thousands in

Japan and was the occasion of the cablegram published in the Japanese newspapers (see page 3).

On this same anniversary, a committee of the Board of Foreign Missions of the Presbyterian Church, coming over from New York, waited upon Dr. and Mrs. Hepburn, and in an address reviewed their labors, from the time when, in 1840, he and his young wife reached Singapore. It was then shown how their lives had run parallel with the whole course of modern Japan's remarkable history. Some of the things said may have tried severely the Doctor's modesty, yet, as he had, by his record, brought the infliction upon himself, he had to take it. The address — couched in choice language and chaste terms and rich in sympathy — began as follows:

"HONORED AND BELOVED FATHER:

"We are mindful of the habitual modesty, with which you regard yourself as an unprofitable servant, but illustrious examples of success are a part of the moral and spiritual assets of civilization and of the Redeemer's kingdom. The church therefore, and the nation, nay, and more than all perhaps the Japanese nation, must be permitted to estimate your work by relative standards. You have been blessed with a most versatile career, for which you and we render God the thanks.

"In Japan you laid your plans at first for thorough work. Foregoing the attractions of the foreign community in Yokohama, you and Mrs.

Hepburn took yourselves to the suburb of Kanagawa, where you found a transient home in an old temple and away from all foreigners, that you might accomplish a real mastery of the language and be in closer and heartier touch with the people whom you aimed to serve. It was by this schooling, that you were prepared to supply the first great Anglo-Japanese dictionary, which, like a golden key, opened the way between the East and West and hastened immensely the progress of civilization."

Then in the address congratulations were offered especially upon the notable record in that sort of missionary service — for the body — which makes the first appeal to a non-Christian people. Resisting the temptation to turn aside for the amassing of personal fortune, Hepburn had wrought wholly as a missionary, without emolument. "Upon the visit of one of our secretaries to Japan in 1874, a prominent foreign resident of Yokohama said to him, 'There is good Dr. Hepburn, who might have made a splendid fortune by his medical profession, still living upon his small salary in that nasty little house down by the canal.'"

The Doctor's zeal in the great work of translating the Bible was noted, and he was pictured as "laboring indefatigably and in all intervals and scraps of time at that great work, as if it were the only one you had in mind. There are those in the Mission House, who well remember the persistent fidelity with which, even on furlough and in the midst of intense summer heat, you toiled at your manuscript and proofs for the printer.

"You were also a preacher in Japan. Though without ordination, you were accustomed to hold Sunday services regularly, in which you lovingly presented the glad tidings of great joy to the listening people."

Reference was made in detail to the Doctor's great influence, social, political and diplomatic, and to the appreciation which he received from prominent Japanese, and quotations were made from the Anglo-Japanese newspapers.

The ability of the natives of Japan was gladly recognized. "No master builder ever had better material to work upon. Mankind is astonished, not only by the military achievements of the Japanese nation, but by the moral attitude, the dignity and honor, and the human spirit of government and people. The nation you found in spiritual darkness seems to have sprung almost at a bound to the high standards of Christian civilization and philanthropy. What we rejoice at, most of all, is the manifest leaven of Christian influence, which appears, and particularly in the high testimony of men prominent in parliament, in the army and navy, and in educational work."

A happy compliment was paid to the "help meet for him," then under the shadow of mental weakness. "How bravely and lovingly did she bear with you the terrible hardships of your early voyages to the mission field, the sore trials of pioneer work among ignorant and degraded people, with almost none of the comforts of our home life, and the hardships and discouragement of trying to overcome the prejudice and hostility which were first encountered. What a flood of sunshine she poured upon you and all about her, through all the days of her youth, and middle life, and even until a very recent period."

On this same birthday, the Book Department of the Z. P. Maruya Company, the great publishers, in Tokyo, sent their congratulations, in a letter dated June 19, 1905: "Inasmuch as we have been honored as publishers of your master work." They added a present, in the form of an embroidered screen, with their cordial good wishes.

In logical sequence, there followed a tribute to the nonagenarian from the American Bible Society; while his Alma Mater, Princeton University, and her sons hastened to do honor to their "oldest living graduate."

The American Bible Society, May 15, 1905, "In view of his preëminent services, as the principal translator of the Japanese Bible" — extended its sincere congratulations, and made record of the fact.

At the commencement exercises of Princeton University, June 14, 1905, Dr. Hepburn was presented with the degree of Doctor of Laws (LL.D.). In the president's Latin salutatory delivered on that occasion the recipient was spoken of as "James Curtis Hepburn, of the class of 1832, now entering his tenth decade, the oldest living graduate of Princeton University."

After outlining his life and work, the address closed with the words, "To-day we tardily and inadequately honor this venerated scholar, translator, physician, and herald of the cross in the Far East."

Later, on the Doctor's ninety-third birthday, the future president of the United States thus addressed him by letter:

PRINCETON UNIVERSITY,
PRINCETON, N. J., March 10, 1908.

PRESIDENT'S ROOM

MY DEAR MR. HEPBURN, — I am about starting west for Chicago, but before doing so must give myself the pleasure of congratulating you on reaching your ninety-third birthday, as I understand you are to do, on Friday next. I hope that you realize the high honor in which you are held by all who know you and all who know of your work, and that you realize in particular the very great pride that all Princeton men have in the life work by which you have won such honorable distinction. It is a real pleasure to have you still with us, and I know that I am expressing the general feeling, when I wish you continued good health and send you a Godspeed in the name of all Princeton men.

With warmest regard,
Faithfully yours,
(Signed) WOODROW WILSON.

DR. J. C. HEPBURN

On October 17, 1906, Dr. Hepburn received word from beyond seas, that he had been elected honorary president of the Princeton Alumni Association of Japan, formed August 1, 1906.

[213]

On January 25, 1909, the mail brought to him a warm letter from the Medical Missionary Conference in session at Battle Creek, Michigan, at which he was not able to be present:

"We unanimously desire to express to you our deep sense of the noble work done by you in both China and Japan."

On October 21, 1909, in Shiloh church, in Yokohama, there was held a service commemorating the fiftieth anniversary of the arrival of Dr. Hepburn in Japan.

Among the speakers were President Ibuka and Rev. H. Yamamoto, who dwelt on the moral and social transformation wrought in a half century.

A commemorative marble tablet, in double form, inscribed in Japanese and English, was unveiled in Dr. Hepburn's honor. In its simplicity and truthfulness, it well represents the modesty and plainness of the man whose memory it is designed to perpetuate.

The English text of this tablet reads:

In commemoration of the arrival of the beloved physician, James Curtis Hepburn, M.D., LL.D., pioneer Presbyterian missionary to Japan, Oct. 18, 1859; by whose efforts this edifice was erected, and by him presented to the Shiloh church for the worship of Shiloh.

To Him shall the obedience of the peoples be.

An address by J. H. Ballagh followed the unveiling of the tablet. He referred to the centurion of whom it was said to Jesus, "He is worthy that thou shouldest

MEMORIAL TABLETS

do this for him; for he loveth our nation, and hath built us a synagogue." He dwelt at some length on Dr. Hepburn's prolonged labors in lexicography and translation, as well as in education, his work being crowned by his appointment as president of the Méiji Gaku-in.

The speaker called attention to the fact that many foreigners and natives had the impression that Dr. Hepburn was a minister of the gospel, as he certainly was, though without the sentimental value of a diploma, and lacking the laying on of hands upon his head — even as did the great apostle to the Gentiles. He, like Paul, was without the "ordination," "holy orders," or any other authorization, except the gift of the Holy Spirit and the will of Christian people. In a word, he was an apostle, that is, a missionary. The "apostolic succession," according to language and history, is a succession of missionaries, and any theory of such a "succession," which discredits Christian experience, the work of the Holy Spirit in the hearts of men, had little value in the Doctor's eyes.

"Dr. Hepburn conducted service, taught a Bible class, and often occupied a pulpit in the absence of the pastor. A further proof of Dr. Hepburn's love of the Japanese nation was his generous gift to the fund for the building of the large dormitory for the students of the Méiji Gaku-in, which was gratefully named after him, and also a professor's house on the same ground."

XXIII

THE TRANSFORMATION OF HALF
A CENTURY

DURING his stay in Japan, Dr. Hepburn saw the birth, growth and banyanlike spreading of the doctrine of Mikadoism, which, in the hands of the bigots, the ignorant, the Chauvinists, and more especially those who used it for personal and selfish ends, has had a blighting effect upon the intellect of Japan, increasing their insular conceit and making them blind opposers of moral progress and real civilization. The doctrine of both the deity and the divinity of the Mikado has undoubtedly been politically serviceable in unifying the Japanese nation and the various tribes and peoples, that have become incorporated in the empire. Yet, also, by the manipulation of the unscrupulous politicians, military and civil, bureaucrats, and men that enjoy the methods of Russia more than of England, Mikadoism has become an engine of oppression as well as of obstruction. In Korea and Formosa, it has often been, in the hands of ignorant policemen and henchmen only too ready to curry favor with their superiors, a means of terrorizing the innocent people, quite equal to the Spanish Inquisition or the Italian Camorra, or Black Hand. In 1912, when military bureaucracy attempted to override the constitution of 1889, the people rose against their oppressors, and struck a blow in favor of democracy.

In other words, Mikadoism has been at once a blessing and a bane, according as it has been used by the unselfish patriot or the selfish schemers. Mikadoism has dwarfed the national intellect, making it too self-centered and insularly narrow, while also paralyzing or sterilizing the nobler aspirations of the nation. It has taught the abominable and false doctrine that Christianity and loyalty are not compatible. In some of the pamphlets and writings of the radical believers in Mikadoism, statements are made and arguments are used that almost pass the bounds of credibility that they could have come from adult men of intellect. It is to be hoped that the Japanese will outgrow this puerile superstition, without in any way endangering the loyalty of the people to their chief ruler, or showing any lack of reverence for the noble line of emperors that has filled the throne.

Too often, the insufferable conceit and puerile dogmatism of pagan Japan has been swelled by unwise foreign flatterers. Possibly even Dr. Barrows and Dr. Charles Cuthbert Hall, had they known the rustic and urban reality of native life as I saw it, might not have so flattered the islanders. One English missionary is reported to have said that "he felt it inappropriate to repeat the Ten Commandments to the Japanese"! Others declare that he put it even more strongly than that — he "thought it an insult" to do so. There are some peculiar people in the world, and so much wiser than their Creator.

A veteran missionary wrote in 1912:

"Dr. Hall emphasized the idea not to Europeanize the Japanese, but to let them have the content of the gospel without its Western form." Good! Yet, "That, too, is easier said than done. The Lord rules in all."

Two great wars on the continent of Asia, in which Japan was a principal actor, were fought during Dr. Hepburn's later years. Occasionally yielding to urgent requests for light upon the subjects uppermost in the public mind, he consented to lecture. His ideas were well worth receiving and pondering, especially when the impressions of Occidentals concerning the Japanese were changing with almost acrobatic rapidity and often lack of rhyme or reason.

From being interesting but amusing "Orientals," "yellow monkeys," "little brown men," etc., etc., as the ignorant and conceited white folks had once described them, the Japanese were suddenly transformed by the newspapers into superhuman heroes. Then again, Americans, who had hitherto patronizingly imagined all "Japs" to be picturesque but harmless, suddenly discovered in them giants and dragons, yes, even the would-be conquerors and enslavers of America. These amazing islanders were

not only drilling in regiments by moonlight in Hawaii
and making kodak pictures of the interior of all our
forts, but seemed actually on the point of crossing
the Pacific to review their victorious legions from the
summit of Bunker Hill, or the Capitol at Washington. So frightfully superhuman had the Japanese
become, that politicians were seized with hysterics.
Legislation, that would distinctly violate our treaties,
and was therefore constructively treasonable, was
threatened in state legislatures. Excited and even
frenzied apostles preached the dire need of a colossal navy. The prospective contractors of navy and
army supplies of steel, powder, shells, beans, pork,
bacon and hard-tack rejoiced. Manufacturers of
war material rubbed their hands in glee.

How heartily we quondam dwellers in Japan did
laugh at the tomfoolery of nations! Yet neither the
shouting brethren at home, nor the diligent scribblers
of Europe — who would most gladly cripple the
Republic, or weaken the islanders — were able
to drag us into war — not even with Portugal or
Mexico.

Dr. Hepburn detested flatterers and never handled
the disgusting commodity of flattery, of which so
much has been dumped upon the Japanese. In
one of his first lectures this master of facts showed
what they had not, and what they had, before the
advent of foreigners. He detailed their great debt
to China. "I may say everything they use, as well
as their laws, form of government, and a large part of

their language and literature, was also derived from the Chinese. It is characteristic of the Japanese that they have invented and originated but little, but have borrowed largely from other nations and improved upon what they borrowed — a striking feature of the nation at the present time. In this respect, they are the opposites of the Chinese."

He called attention to the fact that in the seventeenth century deeds of sale and contract were only valid when they had a clause inserted that the parties at interest did not belong to "the vile Christian sect."

"The peasantry, the largest portion of the population, uneducated and ignorant, like serfs bound to the soil, lived in great poverty, one half or more of the product of their toil going as taxes to their feudal lord.

"The whole nation was given up to licentiousness and the gratification of animal instincts, with no gods higher than deified men, no religion better than Buddhism and idolatry, no morals higher than Chinese Confucianism, without the knowledge of God, or of accountability to a Supreme Being. Without the Bible, without the knowledge of salvation through Jesus Christ, without schools, or any of the improvements or great inventions of modern or Western civilization, they lived a quiet, secluded, torpid and sleepy existence, from which they were suddenly aroused in 1853."

The Doctor believed that the results of the war

WHERE NEW JAPAN WAS BORN
March 4, 1771

with China would be for "great good and to the special advancement of the kingdom of God, not only in the three nations of Japan, Korea and China directly interested, but in all Asia and even in Europe.

"The leaven of Christianity is now slowly but powerfully pervading the Japanese people and we may safely predict that ere many years have elapsed, Japan will be numbered among the Christian nations."

The Doctor noticed that since he left Japan, the prayers and the longings of the missionaries for the past thirty-five years had been answered, for the new treaties (in 1900) gave Japan perfect autonomy and sovereign rights, and opened the country to foreign residence and travel.

"As the success which the Japanese have obtained against the Chinese has been almost entirely the result of Christian civilization, the war will result rather to the advantage of Christianity. . . . The hand of God is particularly manifested in this war, in breaking down the conservatism, bigotry and pride of the Chinese, in opening China to the gospel, as well as to Western civilization. It will revolutionize Korea, reform the government and elevate the people, and in the end will be a blessing to the Japanese, though its immediate effects are attended with much suffering."

After picturing in detail the great changes in Japan, including the use of movable type, daily newspapers, beef, milk, butter, beer, wine, hats, shoes, linen handkerchiefs and foreign clothing, besides the manufacture of sewing machines, clocks, organs, surgical and dental instruments, steam engines and every kind of machinery, he said:

"It is, to be sure, like a new dress [this material civilization] and fits them somewhat awkwardly, but they are rapidly becoming used to it, and will in the end modify it, so as to suit their own ideas and tastes. The result will be a civilization perhaps somewhat peculiar, but more in accordance with their own national taste. But not until they have discarded paganism, turned from idolatry, and built up their civilization upon the basis of the religion of Jesus Christ, will it be homogeneous, stable and enduring."

He said of Shinto: "It has no idols, no sacred books, teaches no moral duties, either to God or to man, has no idea of sin, or human depravity, but has of praying to the *kami*, or gods, with clean hands and bodily purification; believes that the spirits of the dead go to Hades, or the Land of Roots, and speaks of ascending to Ten, or heaven, where the gods dwell. Their gods are all endowed with human bodies and passions, are born and die, are impure, licentious, quarrel, fight, get drunk and perform all kinds of human conduct. Shinto has no monasteries or convents, as the Buddhists have, but, connected with the temples are priestesses, young girls who go through a pantomime of prayer and worship, and of making offerings to the gods. These

IN OLD JAPAN   IN NEW JAPAN

girls are not vestal virgins, but marry when opportunity offers."

On December 15, 1909, S. Kodama, M.D., wrote
him a letter which graphically illustrated the rapid
change in Japan, saying, "My whole country remembers you by your name, 'Hepburn San,' from the
Emperor's household to the common people." Dr.
Kodama had been in the Méiji Gaku-in and was
there inspired to become a medical missionary, working among his countrymen in California and Hawaii
for twenty years or more. At the time of writing he
was then forty-five years old, he rejoiced that his old
father, seventy-four years old, and his uncle sixty-
eight years old, his wife's father and his cousin were
members of the Christian Church, of which he was
at that time acting as Japanese pastor. This was
but one of the many typical changes in family life
in Japan. In the long run the nation will become
Christian by families, rather than by individuals.

Further notable testimonies to the wonderful revolution going on in the life of the Japanese were
given on October 21, 1909, when the members of
Shiloh church held a commemoration service to celebrate the fiftieth anniversary of the arrival of the
Hepburns in Japan. It will be remembered that
this church, both as to edifice and congregation,
owed its existence largely to the labors of Dr. Hepburn. The pastor, Rev. Kanamori, who presided,
introduced Honorable Shimada Saburo, member of
the Imperial Diet in Tokyo, a champion of social

morality, author of an epoch-making book,[1] and one of the most brilliant and forceful editors, authors and orators which modern Japan has produced. He held the tense interest of his audience for over an hour, while reviewing the changes, in political and religious life, during the previous half century, since Drs. Hepburn, Brown and Verbeck had landed in Japan. He contrasted the methods and results of the propagation of Christianity in the sixteenth and in the nineteenth century. He pictured the religious and civil struggles and the agitation for liberty of conscience in Japan, rejoicing that since the beginning of the Méiji era there had been no persecution. In his appeals for still larger and freer social and religious influences, the orator was warmly applauded.

The comment of the reporter of the Japan "Gazette" was this:

> The speaker's rapidity of utterance and steady advance of thought was truly remarkable. If Christianity has done nothing else but develop such a champion for the cause of purity and truth, it has wrought marvels.

During all these years the missionaries had to contend not only against paganism, but against the energy and opposition of hostile aliens. Dr. D. C. Greene, on March 23, 1892, sent to the Japan "Mail" an article in answer to severe criticisms made by some anonymous coward, under the signature of

[1] *Agitated Japan*, New York, 1886. In the original Japanese, *Kaikoku Shimatsu*.

Hard Fact, denouncing the servants of Christ as "uncultured." Of twenty-nine missionaries on the ground, twenty-four were graduates of universities in Europe or America. Of the remaining five, two were laymen, who, by their success, had amply justified their appointment.

Shortly before this date, a Japanese professor in the Imperial University had declared that only three translations worthy of the name had as yet appeared in Japan. These were Senator Nakamura's "Self Help," Mr. Mitsukuri's "Code Napoleon," and the Japanese version of the Bible. Another well-known Japanese had described the last-named version as "unparalleled," while all knew that Dr. Verbeck, whose "version of the Psalms is unexcelled as a faithful and idiomatic translation," had contributed largely to the success of Mr. Mitsukuri. Dr. M. L. Gordon's researches in the field of Japanese Buddhism, and those of Rev. George William Knox, in Chinese Philosophy, were deserving of high praise.

Dr. Greene noted the work of the surgeon, Rev. W. M. Taylor, M.D., of Osaka, who was probably without a superior in Japan, and the scientific observations of Rev. John P. Gulick, Ph.D., of Osaka, so highly praised by G. H. Romeyns, and by Wallace as a profound thinker on subjects usually associated with the name of Darwin, though the main work of missionaries has been expended in work on the Japanese language. As to "international fair play," he said that nearly all the missionaries would rejoice in the abolition of extra-territoriality (which came about in 1900). In the country at large, he said, forty per cent of the Christians were of the samurai class, though the gentry or men of privilege constituted only five per cent of the entire population. Among the Christians in Tokyo, nearly seventy-five per cent were of the gentry class. In one of the churches, two officers of the government held rank directly from the Emperor and twelve held appointments from the Council of State, all Christians. The previous House of Representatives had thirteen Christians and the House of Peers four, while the followers of Jesus held an enviable place in the prefectural assemblies. In one of these, out of sixty members, eight were Christians, from among whom the president was chosen. At this time, the touring missionaries were overwhelmed with invitations to come and preach in new places.

Dr. Greene also showed the vast benefits, physical and moral, of the keeping of the Sabbath day. Native observers had noticed the frequent breakdown of those who toiled in the silk factories, because of excessive hours of labor, that is, from early dawn to ten at night. It was rare to find an operative over thirty years of age — their prolonged diligence, with few intervals of rest, causing an early breakdown of the nervous system, rendering subsequent labor impossible even if life itself were not sacrificed. Christians had really created the public sentiment which brought in legislation making factory life more tolerable. Dr. Greene concluded that "to be one of a company which is able to aid, at so many different points, in the building up of New Japan seems to me a privilege and the work a holy work."

XXIV

THE TOLLING BELL

UNTIL his last days, this lover of Japan was as a watchman waiting for the morning to dawn. He studied the news and reports from the Sunny Isles, and rejoiced at every token of the coming kingdom. In July, 1911, his bodily powers showed signs of speedy collapse, yet he lived until September 21, when after many hours of coma, he breathed his last. By a strange coincidence, Hepburn Hall, in the Méiji College grounds in Tokyo, went up in flames during the dying hours of the man who gave it.

About three hundred persons attended the farewell services in the Brick Church, on September 23, some of those present being Japanese, and one of them an official representative from the Legation in Washington. From its conservatories, sent by the ambassador Baron Chinda, was a wreath of white orchids. Dr. James Riggs, the Doctor's pastor, in treating of his personal acquaintance, spoke of the sweetness and simplicity of his parishioner. Very appropriately the graceful sentences of eulogy were delivered, and the life story of the deceased told with deep

[228]

feeling, by Arthur Judson Brown, D.D., one of the statesmanlike secretaries of the Presbyterian Board of Foreign Missions. Without fulsome praise he touched the exact truth when he said:

"Most of us begin our lives at a time when the work with which we are connected is well under way. The plans are all made and the foundations laid, and we simply continue to work on the lines laid out. Here was a man who found no foundations laid, but who had to make his own plans and lay his own foundations. He was one of the constructive men.

"He thought there were physicians enough already in America. He felt that the place for him was the place that needed him the most, and so he applied for an appointment as missionary. Few had then visited Asia, and those few had not brought back reassuring reports. A great part of Asia could not then be reached. The young physician was thought crazy when he planned to go to one of those unknown lands."

Ninety-six times, according to the old custom of numbering the years, did the church bell toll, as the procession moved from that church to the burial place at Rosedale Cemetery—sweet word coined in Christian love and hope, and meaning "a sleeping chamber." There rests the dust of Dr. Hepburn with that of his wife and children — in the care of the Resurrection and the Life.

Memorial services were held at the Méiji Gaku-in

on September 28, 1911. They were largely attended by students, Christian pastors and foreign friends. Besides speakers from the faculty and from other bodies of Christians, Hon. A. Hattori, Member of Parliament, delivered a noble and touching eulogy of "the man who brought Christian civilization to Japan."

At the close of the service, a large number of "appreciations" of Dr. Hepburn, reprinted from the Japan "Gazette," with his portrait and pictures of the Hepburn Hall — burned on the day of his decease — were distributed, and eagerly sought for. Many of those present visited the scene of the fire, and wondered that so many edifices — including a new recitation hall and a whole row of professors' residences — were saved.

For the enlightenment of those Americans who still cling to the traditional and often baseless stories, supposed to illustrate the lack of Japanese integrity, we may add the fact, that, although the cause of the fire was not yet satisfactorily ascertained, the Japanese insurance companies paid the insurance immediately.

To-day in the beautiful city of the dead, named from the valley of roses, all is bright and fair, with both summer's blooming children and the symbols of Christian faith and hope. In hallowed concord, both nature and art raise their protest of the resurrection hope against the might and mystery of death, even while they recall Christ as Victor. In the days of his flesh on earth, Jesus loved the flowers of the field which his Father had clothed in more than regal beauty. Of the bloom of plant and tree, Dr. Hepburn was all his life a passionate lover. As one looks upon the mounds of the beloved physician and his helpmate, faith makes audible again the words to each, "Well done, good and faithful servant . . . enter thou into the joy of thy Lord."

INDEX

A.B.C.F.M., 25
Abeel, David, 49, 50, 57, 63
Adams, Will, 176
Alexander, J. Addison, 14
Allen, Horace N., 153
Allen, Young J., 99, 100, 153
American Bible Society, 133, 212
Americans in the Far East, 44, 48, 53, 54, 56, 77
Anti-christian edicts, 145
Apostles, 215
Apostles' Creed, 182
Appenzeller, Henry Gerhart, 8
Armstrong, Richard, 21
Asia, 229
Asiatic Society of Japan, 204
Assam, 141, 166
Assassination, 157
American Tract Society, 156

Bailey, Rev., 180
Ballagh, Rev. James H., 141, 172, 177, 179, 181, 195, 214
Banzai, 165
Baptists, 141
Barrows, Dr., 217
Batavia, 47, 48, 131
Berry, Dr. J. C., 124
Bettelheim, Dr., 140
Bible, 65, 101, 137–149, 154, 160–167, 188, 192, 206
Bible dictionary, 157
Bible training school, 153
Birds, 34, 35, 40, 62, 163
Blossoms, 150
Books, 224, 225
Boston, 26, 27, 43, 57

Brick Presbyterian Church, 200, 228
Bridgeman, Dr., 63, 195
British and Foreign Bible Society, 140
Brown, Arthur Judson, 229
Brown, Nathan, 141, 142, 147, 166, 167
Brown, Rev. Samuel Robbins, 8, 52, 74, 79, 139, 141, 172, 179, 180, 190, 207, 224
Browning, Robert, 195
Buddhism, 145, 148, 149, 169–171, 220, 225
Burgess and Burdick, 179

Calcutta, 179
Calvinism, 28, 97, 98
Camoens, 57
Campbell Hall, 202
Canton, 58
Carrothers, Rev. C., 181
Cats, 116
Cemetery, Rosedale, 229
Chamberlain, Basil Hall, 127
China, 53–63, 159, 219, 221
Chinda, Baron, 228
Chinese, 25, 46, 47, 51, 64, 130, 225
Chinese language, 96, 139, 142
Christianity, 69, 71, 74, 145, 187, 220, 221, 224, 226
Church Missionary Society, 147
Churches, 156, 178–182
Church of Christ in Japan, 182, 185, 186, 188
Civil war, 170, 177
Civilization, 222

[233]

INDEX

INDEX

INDEX

INDEX

INDEX